A DIARY O

First published in 2024 by Wordville
(info@wordville. net)

A Diary of War & Theatre © Richard Nelson, 2024

All rights reserved.

You may not copy, store, distribute, transmit, reproduce or otherwise make available this publication (or any part of it) in any form, or binding or by any means (print, electronic, digital, optical, mechanical, photocopying, recording or otherwise), without the prior written permission of the publisher. Any person who does any unauthorized act in relation to this publication may be liable to criminal prosecution and civil claims for damages.

ISBN: 9781399991964

10 9 8 7 6 5 4 3 2 1

Richard Nelson

A DIARY OF WAR & THEATRE

MAKING THEATRE IN KYIV, SPRING 2024

Wordville

RICHARD NELSON

RICHARD NELSON has directed over twenty of his plays, as well as those by Chekhov and Turgenev. His plays include *The Michaels, Illyria, The Gabriels* (*Hungry, What Did You Expect?* and *Women of a Certain Age*), *The Apple Family Plays* (*That Hopey Changey Thing, Sweet and Sad, Sorry* and *Regular Singing*), *Conversations in Tusculum, Nikolai and the Others, Farewell to the Theatre, An Actor Convalescing in Devon, Goodnight Children Everywhere* (Olivier Award Best Play), *Two Shakespearean Actors* (Tony Nomination, Best Play), *Some Americans Abroad* (Olivier Nomination, Best Comedy), and others. His musicals include *James Joyce's The Dead* (with Shaun Davey, Tony Award Best Book of a Musical, Tony nomination for Best Musical); his screenplays include *Hyde Park on Hudson* (Roger Michell, director). With Richard Pevear and Larissa Volokhonsky, he has co-translated plays by Chekhov, Gogol, Turgenev, and Bulgakov. He is an Honorary Associate Artist of the Royal Shakespeare Company and recipient of the PEN/Laura Pels 'Master Playwright' Award. He recently directed his play, *Notre Vie Dans l'Art* at the Théâtre du Soleil, in Paris, translated by Ariane Mnouchkine. He lives in Upstate New York.

"To find a form that accommodates the mess,
that is the task of the artist now."

Samuel Beckett

TABLE OF CONTENTS

FOREWORD Oksana Prybish	1
INTRODUCTION	3
DIARY	11
REVIEWS OF 'CONVERSATIONS IN TUSCULUM'	151
EPILOGUE	155
APPENDIX	165
'CONVERSATIONS IN TUSCULUM' Scene-by-Scene Synopsis	167
PHOTOGRAPHS	168
ACKNOWLEDGEMENTS	169

FOREWORD

WHEN GUESTS COME to a Ukrainian theatre, especially from abroad, everyone here is incredibly excited. Who knows where this tradition came from—whether it is the result of living behind the Iron Curtain or something rooted in Ukrainian identity and mindset.

Meeting, talking, and working with Richard Nelson during this war became a gift for the theatre company. Probably, because he knows how to listen. In Ukraine, there is no real tradition of going to a psychologist, so friends, relatives, and colleagues witness all our emotions, impressions, and worries. When a person works in the theatre, especially on a production, we literally live there, and so only our colleagues become the ones left to listen to us.

Perhaps this ability to listen, remember, and feel is the quality of a good theatre professional, especially a playwright, especially someone like Richard who understands that conversations about life and daily routine often hide the pain, dreams, hopes, and tragedy of a nation.

When our creative team first read his play about Ancient Rome, and tried to draw parallels to the present, not everyone understood the connection and so there were questions about why the theatre needed to produce it. At the Theatre on Podil everything is fueled by mutual passion, which is usually generated by the passion of the director. And so after several introductory conversations with Richard no one involved in the process wanted to leave. And—despite a setting in the distant past, within a totally different world, despite having to work during such a difficult time—after the premiere, we did not want to let Richard go; he had begun as our guest but had become a dear part of our family at the Theatre on Podil.

Any collaboration with professionals from abroad, including working on a play, opens a door to a new dimension for the Ukrainian theatre, for our theatre, and to an adventure and a journey. And we do love to travel, even if we cannot cross the border of Ukraine just yet.

With warmth and gratitude for Richard's patience and experience,

Oksana Prybish
Head of the Literary and Dramatic Department of the
Kyiv Academic Drama Theatre on Podil

INTRODUCTION

THE BACKGROUND

SUMMER, 2020

IN THE MIDST of the Covid pandemic, I began to write a play based upon a story I had long wanted to explore, and one I had been researching for years. As the characters were all Russian I hoped to produce this play in Russia in Russian. My friend, the translator, Larissa Volokhonsky, offered to translate; and I wrote to a famous Russian director about my idea. He was intrigued. I then wrote the play over several months, sent him the translation in early 2021, received his wildly enthusiastic response, and he urged me to quickly come to St. Petersburg (in the midst of the pandemic) to discuss the play and production at his theatre.

SUMMER, 2021

Along with Larissa as my guide (she is a native of St. Petersburg) I flew to Russia. The director and I talked for days about the play, but eventually it became clear that we had a fundamental disagreement about the story. So this production never happened.

However, I had a conversation during this visit which I would later remember and which would become the source of this book and my diary: a woman working in this theatre mentioned an earlier play of mine called *Conversations in Tusculum* and how she felt it would be an important play to do in Russia today. That is, she said, until she read the last line. The play is set in 45 BCE, the summer before the Ides of March, as Brutus, Cassius, and Cicero try and convince themselves that they can 'manage' the dictator, Caesar. They learn they can't, they betray and humiliate themselves, and the last line of the play is: "He must die."

The play does not address the plotting of the assassination, but rather focuses on the summer before, as smart, 'decent' people continue to believe in their abilities to handle and control a dictator or all-powerful politician. Like all of my plays, what interested me were the people; and here I found characters who were complex, confused, lost, and self-questioning.

I didn't give up on my Russian play. I next reached out to the artistic director of an important theatre in Moscow; he too responded favorably to the play. He too urged me to come quickly to Russia (still in the midst of the pandemic). We met and agreed that we both saw the play the same way; we set dates for the production in the next fall. Later that winter, as is the custom in Russian theatre, he read my play to his company of actors. The morning after the reading (I wasn't there) I was sent a series of photos of the actors listening, laughing, focused on what was the first time my play was ever read out loud. But along with the photos, came this message: "something bad has just happened."

The date of the reading: Feb. 23, 2022. The next day, the morning the photos were sent, Russia invaded Ukraine.

A SURPRISE INVITATION

It was in the first week of the war (or 'full-scale invasion' as I have learned to call it, as Russia had already invaded Ukraine in 2014) that I remembered the woman in the famous director's theatre talking about my play set in 45 BCE, and how it would be an important play to do in Russia today. I saw, through her eyes, how the play portrays the compromises, betrayals, desperation, impotence of those who have allowed Putin to rise to the position and power he now holds and wields. I asked Larissa to translate the play into Russian and together we set about trying to locate a theatre to produce it—in Russian, with Russian actors, but obviously not in Russia. We reached out to Russian-speaking theatres in Lithuania, Latvia, Estonia, Georgia, and Israel. All expressed interest, but something kept them from committing to a production; I suspect they felt a tentativeness as guests in these countries. Larissa then happened to meet a Ukrainian actor in Paris, where she lives; told him about the play, gave him the Russian translation, which he then took back to Kyiv.

On July 27, 2023, I received a WhatsApp message:

Dear Mr. Nelson. I am a project manager of the Theatre on Podil in Kyiv. Theatre director Bohdan Benyuk told me that you had expressed a desire to stage your play 'Conversations in Tusculum' in our theatre. If you still want to, we would be glad to discuss, for example in Zoom, all the details:
dates, funding, team etc.
Kind regards.

I had already heard that there was some sort of interest in the play at a theatre in Kyiv; though that was pretty much all I knew. I now Googled this theatre, Theatre on Podil, and learned that it was considered one of the most important theatres in Kyiv, in an historic district; that it played in repertory, has a fairly large resident acting company, a newish proscenium theatre with about 250 seats, and a smaller 'second' theatre. Bohdan Benyuk, I learned, is one of Ukraine's most honored actors and, I found out much later, a politician. I obviously didn't read the email as closely as I might have, because the 'surprise offer' I would soon receive was clearly already there. We scheduled our Zoom for August 3rd.

I saw on the theatre's website that Benyuk had a performance on the 3rd; and so our Zoom was scheduled for shortly after his show came down. I asked Larissa to be on the call as well—though she doesn't speak Ukrainian, I knew that everyone there also speaks Russian. So at the end of the call, were I confused about anything said, I could confer with her.

Bohdan is a warm, large man, with an open face, full of enthusiasm—very much the actor. After a few polite greetings he got right to the point: would I be interested in directing my play at his theatre? He proposed a nine-week rehearsal period sometime in the spring, 2024. I was taken aback; until then I had thought I would at most get to Kyiv for three maybe four days to catch the opening. He explained that my directing would make an 'impression' in Kyiv at this time, by which he meant during the war, and so would become some sort of an 'event' in the Kyiv theatre world. A nine-week residency to create a production, in Ukrainian, with Ukrainian actors from the theatre's company, would make a statement of support, is how I heard what he was saying. During the war. I agreed.

THE NEXT STEPS

I said I would not accept any fee or royalties, and would look to friends and foundations to help pay my travel and living expenses.

Even before our Zoom, the theatre had commissioned a translation into Ukrainian. Once I had agreed to direct, I kept asking, month after month, how the translation was coming and when could I see it? At the time I had a project manager overseeing this, then that changed and Oksana, the head of the drama department, took over. For my entire time in Kyiv, she would be the person I worked closest with. I finally received the translation sometime in December.

I showed it to Larissa, who is able to read some Ukrainian, and as she had already translated it into Russian, she knew the play well. She was shocked, horrified actually, because this translation was terrible—things had been added, rewritten, my ordinary language became a very heightened theatrical language, whole passages had been completely misunderstood.

The translator didn't seem to have a command of English. As one of the most esteemed professional translators alive today, Larissa was angry and offended by what she called "a real hack job." She took it personally and set about making the translation right. She engaged a young and talented Ukrainian woman in Paris to help. I used some of the money given to support my travel to pay this young woman; Larissa worked for free. They worked hard and delivered a new translation just weeks before rehearsals began. Only then could the actors read the play and learn what their parts were like. The translation was still rough of course; there hadn't been enough time to do a thorough review; the urgent goal being to correct the most heinous mistakes.

I was assigned a set designer based in Munich; a smart, interesting mind with a fine portfolio. I explained that I wanted the set to be simple, only furniture, nothing else. Over Zoom, he worried if "the Theatre on Podil knows what to expect" from my kind of minimalist work—with a focus on people talking to each other, and where there is little obvious drama or conflict. He said their audiences were used to something else, something more visual, and so he was worried. His concern concerned me and so I wrote to the theatre, and got this quickly back:

> *Mr. Benyuk understood your conception from the very beginning... Obviously it will be a challenging process, but I have no doubt that we'll handle it and gain valuable experience.*

I sent the theatre a series of questions to ask potential actors who wished to be seen for my play; their answers (in Ukrainian) were videotaped—this was how I auditioned. They were mostly personal questions: about their backgrounds, how they got into theatre, roles they loved and roles they hated, their families, their daily lives today, and so forth. Of course I couldn't understand what they said; but I could hear their voices, how they moved; whether they were 'acting' or just 'talking.' I watched these videos many times before selecting my six actors. One did speak English, and in her video she said directly to me—

Richard, you should know how valuable it will be for you to come to Kyiv at this time and direct your play; how meaningful it would be for me and others; a gesture that we will remember.

THE WAR

"Is it safe?" I was asked this many times by my family, friends, colleagues; my agents joked about buying me a bulletproof vest and helmet. The US State Department urged Americans not to visit Ukraine, and if they couldn't be dissuaded then to leave samples of their DNA at home, so their remains could be identified.

Others were less concerned; friends from the Paris theatre where I had just been working, the Théâtre du Soleil, had spent two weeks in Kyiv the previous Spring, and they told me to be careful, but that they had felt safe. The Kyiv theatre booked me into a hotel around the corner from the theatre; I saw on the hotel's website a video of their bomb shelter. I brought extra external batteries for my computer and phone; I packed clothes for both winter and spring. I bought a small voice recorder, because everyone told me, "you have to keep a diary."

WHAT WAS I HOPING FOR?

A play with characters who fail to 'tame' a despot and so are caught in delusion and humiliation presented in front of an audience that is in the midst of a war, an invasion, led by just such a despot; I think I hoped for some kind of visceral conversation between audience and play—a conversation about what is happening today, there, just outside that theatre, to that audience; a conversation that would be immediate, true, alive, and full of meaning.

BEFORE DEPARTING

I read this on the theatre's website (roughly translated by A.I.):

> *If air raid would be announced, all spectators and theatre staff must follow to the shelter. After the signal to cancel the danger, we will continue to play the play. In case the alarm lasts for more than one hour, we will play the play on the morning of the next working day, so that everyone can get home safely before curfew.*
> *By supporting the theatre, you are investing in the future.*
> *Thank you for staying with us.*

A LITTLE ABOUT THE PLAY: 'CONVERSATIONS IN TUSCULUM'

There are eight scenes and six characters, nearly all of whom are related: BRUTUS, PORCIA, CASSIUS, CICERO, SERVILIA, and SYRUS. A scene-by-scene synopsis is included in the appendix.

The entire play takes place in a room in Brutus' Tusculum villa, around a table. Rome and its empire are in flux; Caesar's dictatorship has begun. Brutus and Cassius share their ambiguous feelings about being pardoned by Caesar after fighting against him. Cicero mourns the death of his beloved daughter. As the summer progresses, Cicero attempts to convince Brutus to have patience, and that all is not lost. Caesar surprises Brutus, summoning him in the middle of the night to his camp, where Brutus is encouraged to think that he and Cassius can now have influence over Caesar. This leads to their humiliation and their betrayal of each other and of themselves. At the end of this summer Brutus presents a short play to his guests, a monologue, performed by a houseguest, an actor. It concludes:

He who takes away our country. Our Republic. Pits us against ourselves. He who takes away our freedom and our rights. He who takes away our pride in ourselves and in each other, takes away our moral purpose and resolve. He who corrupts what we cherish. Who divides us to conquer us, who attempts to crown himself and his family 'name', he—must die.

A DIARY OF WAR & THEATRE

Sunday, March 3rd, 2024.
7:45pm:

I begin this diary of my visit to Kyiv. The first time I have kept a diary since I was a teenager. My plan is to talk into a voice recorder, and over time transcribe these entries.

I am on the night train, Warsaw to Kyiv; an 18-hour trip. I have now been on it for two hours. 16 hours more to go. I am alone in a small, tight compartment, maybe seven feet by six feet; with three beds, one on top of the other. Fortunately I am not tall, and fortunately Oksana at the Theatre on Podil suggested I buy three train tickets, one for each bed, and so would have the entire compartment to myself.

There's a small table that lifts up to reveal a sink, and a notice not to drink the water.

The middle 'bed' is folded against the wall; the upper is quite high up and there's a little metal ladder for climbing to it. I'll stay on the bottom one; my bags are all over the floor.

I've been told that at some point in the night we will stop at the border, where I will hand over my passport. And the train then will be lifted up, so that the wheels can be shifted to a new track gauge. Ukraine's railroads have a different gauge than Poland and the rest of Europe; they have the same gauge as Russia's. I have heard that they hope to change this.

Larissa is with me for the first week, to help with the translation; she too has bought three tickets and is in her own compartment next to mine. She's already decided to go bed. I am lying on the bed, reading a paperback book I just bought in Paris; Andrey Kurkov's *Diary of an Invasion*, about the first weeks of the 'full-scale invasion' of Ukraine.

We are pulling into some station now; I have no idea where I am; all is dark outside.

I have food that I bought at a small, crowded grocery in the Warsaw train station, because there is no café car on this train. I bought yogurt, salad, pretzels, water, and a big, too big, bottle of orange juice.

I plan to try and do some work, preparation on the play, because when we arrive in Kyiv tomorrow a little after noon, I'll be taken to the hotel, and then at four o'clock I will meet my actors and start rehearsal.

12.30pm Polish time / 1:30am Ukrainian time:

I was asleep, woken up by the conductor who said something I didn't understand and then left, leaving my door open. I heard him continue down the hallway, knocking on other compartments, waking up other passengers. The train had stopped. I heard voices outside.

I had jumped up, taken out my earplugs and put on my glasses and now sit waiting.

A short time later:

Two Polish soldiers or guards came in, asking, in English, for my passport. I gave it to them, one opened it, looked it over and they took it away. About an hour later one of the soldiers returned it.

I heard banging; metal against metal—the changing of the train wheel gauge for Ukraine.

A female Ukrainian soldier then came in, she too wanted my passport; she too looked it over. When asked how long I would be in Ukraine, and I replied about nine weeks, she stopped what she was doing and looked me in the eye. I then showed her the contract from the theatre that I was told to bring with me, just for this. She read it over.

She again looked closely at me, but this time she was smiling. As she handed me back my passport, she reached to shake my hand.

I think she very much approved of my coming.

I am in Ukraine.

WEEK ONE:

Monday, March 4th.
7:31 am:

I wake up and take my first look at this country; we are going through a forest. During the night I woke up a number of times— the banging when they changed the track gauge went on for hours. But eventually I slept. There is something about sleeping on a train, in a bed, with the rhythmic sound of the tracks… (I'd traveled this way back in the States a number of times in the '80s, going from my home in New York State to Chicago, and fondly remember those trips.)

Outside another forest, this one of birch trees.

A little later:

I Googlemapped to see where we are. We are going past or through something called Tunnel of Love.

Now we are going through a village—with the gold dome of an Orthodox Church. We are in farm country.

Monday, March 4th & Tuesday, March 5th.

I didn't record anything more this day or the next. I was overwhelmed. It would take a while for this diary to become part of my routine.

Larissa and I were met at the train station by Oksana and Yevhen, the managing director. There were crowds of people meeting the train. We drive to our hotel, which is very near the theatre; up a hill along a winding cobblestone street with a large Orthodox Church at the top, in one of Kyiv's most historic districts.

I don't recall my first impressions of Kyiv—and I don't know what I had been expecting.

I met my six actors who I had only seen on video. We gathered in the small second stage, where I had asked to do my play. It had been the ballroom of a large private house. The main theatre is next door. I chose this small space so I could play partially 'in the round' and without a set. This is also a very intimate room, which I like.

A photographer took photos—these would soon go on the theatre's Facebook page. I met Bohdan Benyuk in person; I gave a brief summary of my approach to theatre to my company—"I am an actor-centric director;" as opposed to a director-centric or design-centric director. My interest is in characters and the relationships between characters, as opposed to conveying any vision of my own, or having any images I have in mind that

I wish to create. Everything that we will do, I explain, should come from the actor and be discovered in the characters and their relationships. And nothing else should get in the way of this. I say that I know this isn't a common approach in today's theatre, but I find, unsurprisingly, that once my actors understand that I mean to work this way, they find it empowering.

Tired from the trip, and anxious about beginning, this day and the next remain a blur.

Only much later, on my last full day in Kyiv, nine weeks later, would I learn that there was much anxiety and concern in this room; and questions about me and my motives. Who is this American? Why is he here? What does he want?

Wednesday, March 6th.

I just experienced my first air raid siren/alert. I get a notice from an app on my phone to seek shelter. I go down the six flights of stairs to the hotel's shelter; a couple of men join me there, but others don't. Larissa wrote that she was having breakfast and the people in the restaurant told her not to bother because it was "a warning from far away." I am very happy to go down, it only lasts about 15 or 20 minutes. The shelter is fairly nice, with blankets, water, magazines, chairs and table; the hotel Wi-Fi works here so I will remember to take my computer next time. It was a little cold so I will also remember to bring a jacket. It was good practice, a good learning experience. They seem well organized, in terms of the app on my phone. At the end of the alert, with the 'all-clear', a voice says "May the Force be With You." So we are in Star Wars land.

I'll write more about rehearsal, which is going well. Pleased with my actors. Pleased with what we are talking about. But I'll save that for later; I wanted to record this now.

Saturday, March 9th.

Yesterday was eventful; a rare Friday day off and Oksana organized a tour of one of the major historic sites in Kyiv, St. Sophia's Church. An English-speaking guide was waiting for us. Extraordinary church, dating back to the 11th century; with a rich history.

A lovely day, the sun was out. I took a walk in the morning, down the hill; saw a little bit more of Kyiv.

We had the first production meeting, with designers and others; everyone is amazed (and some are obviously pleased) that I want/need so little for my production. I explained how I wanted to focus on the actors without anything distracting from them, from people. So no set; clothes that are contemporary but which do not draw attention; sound cues to connect scenes; no video; only furniture and basic/simple props.

Dinner with my assistant director, and Arman, an actor from Paris who was just in my play at the Théâtre du Soleil. He is now visiting Kyiv and helping me with rehearsals—he speaks

Ukrainian. It is gift to have him here. We have an early dinner at a kind of Ukrainian-style fast-food restaurant, down the hill in the large square with a big Ferris Wheel; crowds of people in the streets; I saw young people dancing in the street, just enjoying themselves. I came across this about the restaurant in the *Kyiv Independent* (an English-language online newspaper):

> *An invention of the Soviet Union's founding father Vladimir Lenin, the stolovaya (called yidalnia in Ukrainian) was meant to control scarce resources and 'liberate' women from the kitchen by freeing them to pursue industrial occupations.*
>
> *Stolovayas were ubiquitous in the USSR, where recipes were standardized and dispersed across the union making dining in a stolovaya a nearly identical experience from Kyiv to Tashkent to Vladivostok.*
>
> *Ukraine's buffet-style chain Puzata Khata (meaning 'potbellied house' in Ukrainian) rose from the stolovaya's enduring popularity throughout the Soviet Union, blending with it home-style Ukrainian dishes beloved among the local population.*
>
> *The Kyiv-Donbas Development Group opened the first Puzata Khata restaurant on October 16th, 2003, in the historic Bessarabka area of central Kyiv, where it still is today.*

An alive place, Kyiv. No visible sense of war, except for sandbags around a few official buildings. As we came down the steep stairs from the restaurant, a man with one leg slowly pulled himself up, with great effort, along the railing. Arman quietly said—"the war." So, of course, there are hints.

During our tour this morning of St. Sophia's, Oksana talked about growing up in Bucha, the town devastated by Russians in the first months of the war, and how she and her parents had left at the start of the war. She only hinted at the atrocities that took place there at that time. She told me more about my assistant director and that he had worked for several years in a theatre in Donetsk in the Donbas. At dinner I asked him about this; he said that the wealthiest theatre in Ukraine had been there and they had hired him right out of school. He said how he disliked many things about it and that many of his students were pro-Russian. Oksana talked about actors escaping from Mariupol and about the theatre there, which had been bombed; about an actor from the Theatre on Podil's company, a brilliant musician as well as actor, who had volunteered and had died in the past few months. His coffin, she said, was brought to the theatre and laid out in the lobby.

I get to bed early and wasn't asleep long before an alert goes off; around 9:55pm. At first I was the only one in the shelter, then the door opened and there was Larissa. I was very pleased to see her; at the last alert she hadn't come down, having met some maids who told her "oh, we don't do that anymore." I told her that I had promised Richard, her husband, that I would try and look after her. So I was happy to see her in the shelter. The alert didn't last long and once again it signed off with "May the Force Be With You."

I spent a good hour on making a rehearsal schedule, which is complicated here. There are some 30 to 40 plays in repertory in the two theatres and they change every day; so with my actors all in other shows, it is difficult to keep track of who is available to rehearse and when. If someone has a show at night (which isn't the night, as the performances start at 6pm because of the curfew) they then can't rehearse in the afternoon. I have nine weeks of rehearsal, but it is more like only four or five when you add up the hours I can have with all my actors.

Today, Saturday, again rehearsal. Day off is Monday. I don't think we'll rehearse tomorrow, Sunday afternoon; there are just too many actor conflicts. Tomorrow, I may go to see one of their plays.

Sunday, March 10th.

Last night, 1:25am the air-raid alert went off. Then—an increased air alert which lasted about half an hour; again met Larissa down in the hotel's shelter. We were the only two.

Read this morning that last night Ukraine downed 35 of 38 Shahed-type drones launched from Crimea into all sorts of districts including Kyiv. Kyiv we know has the best anti-missile system going, so it is the safest place when these attacks occur.

Ready to complete the week of rehearsals this morning, having worked through, talked through, the entire play around the table. After rehearsal, seeing their production of *Oedipus* in the afternoon. A beautiful sunny day in Kyiv.

WEEK TWO:

Tuesday, March 12th.
8:30 am:

I just had breakfast in the hotel's dining room: yogurt, fruit, orange juice, toast, and coffee. Today in rehearsal will begin staging the play. We'll start with the Prologue and Scene 1. I spent a few hours yesterday by myself moving furniture around in the theatre, sorting out where I wanted things, to create 'my space.' I am pleased with how it all looks, how it feels; a good room, good acoustics. Because this 'theatre' was originally the ballroom of a private historic house, it brings its own unique characteristics, such as a door in one wall. Most of my entrances and exits will use this door.

Yesterday, we have number five and number six air alerts; the first in the late afternoon, when I was just about to WhatsApp with Cindy, my wife, which I do every day. I went down to the shelter, and was again the only person there. Number six was late last night; woke me up around 12:30; again I was alone. Both were quite short, the second only about ten minutes, but it did wake me, so I was up for a while, thinking.

All good in rehearsal; pleased with my actors; they seem interested in working with me, excited to have the focus on them as actors, and not being pawns in a show or dressing for a production. The actor/the human being in front of the audience/other human beings—this for me is the essence of theatre.

I saw my first show in Ukrainian, *Oedipus Rex*, on Sunday in the large stage at Theatre on Podil. The house was full. Production not really to my taste, overly busy set, a lot of declaiming as if that is how Greek or classic plays should be done. At the curtain call, the actor playing Oedipus raised his hands for quiet and spoke directly to the audience in a voice that was simple and human, unlike the one he used during the play. Arman, sitting next to me, translated what he said; it was a patriotic speech and he ended with "we wait for Washington." [During most of my time in Kyiv, the US House of Representatives fought with itself over passing a bill for much needed military aid for Ukraine.]

That is how my visit has been so far; you're in your life, you're in your zone, doing your thing and suddenly this war rises up and grabs you by the throat. I got to the theatre to see the show quite early, sat in the lobby, where there was a 'presentation' by the younger actors in the company celebrating Taras Shevchenko, a 19th-century Ukrainian poet and artist. It was his birthday. His drawings and paintings were projected onto a big screen, the actors read from his poems, one actress sang a song that was based upon a poem. You felt the passion, or perhaps given the war, the need to define themselves, or is it 'celebrate' themselves, and their country and their country's culture. This comes up everywhere, in every way. Yesterday afternoon, I had lunch up the hill at a beautiful contemporary Ukrainian restaurant, where each dish, each ingredient of each dish, as it was pointedly explained to me, came from somewhere in Ukraine. "This is how Ukraine does this, this is how Ukraine does that..." The need to define itself. It feels like I am watching a country try and define itself.

We continue in rehearsal to have conversations about my play and how it might connect to Russia, the war, and Putin. I look forward to continuing these; and even more with audiences. I'm anxious to see an audience response, how they relate to the play, how it touches them, or if it hits them, or something else.

I will head to the rehearsal room early today—I have marked out, walked out, the dimensions of the theatre space, and will reconstruct those dimensions in the rehearsal room, with the furniture. I'll do that before anyone else arrives; then begin rehearsal earlier than usual, at 10am.

8pm:

Long day of rehearsal. I spent the early morning alone in the rehearsal room, setting up the room to reflect the theatre, with seats around, and with the furniture in place. Began to put the play on its feet, which was difficult as always, but I think everyone is on board with what I am hoping to do. We made some progress with the first scene; and some very good progress with the second. We'll keep plugging ahead. Two air alerts during rehearsal today; so we continued to rehearse down in the lobby, which is the theatre's shelter, doing what we could. These actors are used to it, just part of the life of putting on a play here right now.

These are now my seventh and eighth air alerts since I've been here, in little more than a week. I start to understand what people have been living with day after day. In rehearsal, at one point one actor started to cry—something in the play, a description by

Cassius of a brutal war touched a nerve, I think. "You think you are strong," she said, "and then you accept it." She said friends from abroad say to her, "oh, you must be so strong," and she says, "not really, we just have no choice." She said, "you think you are on top of it, and then something even more awful happens." She then mentioned the Azov soldiers, the famed defenders in the siege of Mariupol, how the Russians, after capturing them, blew them up. All of this is right below the surface of everything we're doing, working on this play.

I am very thankful to be here at this time.

Wednesday, March 13th.
9am:

I am responding to a text by a close friend, an actor who has been in many of my plays in the States:

> *Dear J. You ask about rehearsals: they are going well. The actors are excited to have 'the actor' put at the heart of the process and production. They have talked about being 'told' by directors where to stand and how to speak. As you know well that is not my process. So we are having fun. Lots of laughs; and real smart input. We worked for a week around the table— going through the play line by line, for both sense and to check on the translation. Yesterday we began to be on our feet. Hard work as always at this stage, and fairly broad sketching, but I think we have started on the right foot. They know what I am after, and it excites them. The war comes up all the time, as this play is so connected to it. One actress teared up over a speech. It's an extraordinary meshing of play and place. It's a beautiful city. And yesterday it snowed. And so even more beautiful. Full of magic. The theatre is across the street from Mikhail Bulgakov's home, where he grew up, and set his novel, 'The White Guard',*

*and even some of 'The Master and Margarita'. Someone has
poured red paint across his plaque—because he was Russian,
though he was born and raised in Kyiv. The museum is closed,
but I have been offered a private tour. A very rich, complex
place. That's it for now, off to rehearsal.
Much love, xx*

Thursday, March 14th.
5:20am:

Air-raid alert and so I headed down to the shelter. I was woken up out of a dream: a theatre dream. I was putting on a play and it wasn't going well. People were saying that the audience would never understand it.

One other person came into the shelter; hardly anyone else comes in, except at the theatre where my actors have to follow me. I guess Kyivans are just tired of it or used to it; I can only imagine how difficult it would be if you had children woken up in the middle of the night, then trying to get them and yourself back to sleep. The pressure is not just physical but obviously also psychological. Why bother actually bombing something or someone as long as you can get an alert going and wake people up? Deprive them of sleep.

Later that day:

An incident in rehearsal yesterday: one of my actresses does a huge amount of work outside the theatre and outside of acting; she owns a farm, runs a bed and breakfast, founded a school, etc. She told me this story:

She was in a fish market, buying some fish, a place she goes to all the time. Besides being an actress and many other things, she is a well-known cook— she's had a cooking show on television, and authored six cookbooks. A man in a tattered military uniform came into the market, looking very disheveled and confused. He went to the fish counter, grabbed a piece of fish with his hands, and began to chew on it without saying a word, and without paying. She said it was salted fish, so I guess a kind of lox. He seemed quite aggressive and that scared the other customers. The owner asked the man what he wanted, but the man just kept eating the fish with his hands down to the bones. Then he angrily said, "you think you are scared now, why don't you go to war and fight?" And he walked out of the shop. She wrote this story up on her Facebook page—she has a great many followers and I guess is a kind of influencer. Her intention was to talk about the soldiers coming back from fighting carrying a great deal of stress and emotional problems, and how there is little help for them now. But what came across to a number of people was that she was criticizing this soldier for eating with his hands, which of course was what he'd been doing in the front lines. She was criticized for being privileged and elitist and for looking down at someone, a soldier, a hero, because of his manners. The criticism went viral; there have even been death threats against her and her children. She is very upset by it. She kept pointing out that she does a great deal of volunteer work for the army; she brings soldiers to her farm every weekend to relax, to be around her animals.

9:30pm:

Besides the two air alerts already mentioned, there was a third in the midst of rehearsal around 11:30am. We tried to go down to the lobby, the theatre's shelter, but another play is being rehearsed there, *A Midsummer Night's Dream*. We hung out in a sort of canteen/café area just above the lobby; there was a brief discussion about whether this was safe, because it had windows. It was decided this was safer than the rehearsal room, so that's where we stayed. One of my actresses, who follows everything happening on Telegram, said about the alert, "this looks serious." After 45 minutes there was the all-clear. Another part of Ukraine was attacked today, there were casualties; but not Kyiv or near Kyiv.

Rehearsal was interesting, as always: we're finding our way; very character-based as my work always is now, which the actors are obviously enjoying and appreciating. During a coffee break, one actress showed us a photo on her phone that a girl had put on Facebook of the devastation of her village, not far from Kharkiv. My actress said she had reached out to this girl, who now had no place to go, and had offered to bring her to her home. It turned out that this village is where our young stage manager grew up and where her father still lives. Looking at these photos, the young stage manager began to cry. My actress said to me: "you probably don't want to hear about our stories."

The war gets closer, not by miles but by emotions. As my actors relax with me and begin to share their concerns, I begin to see what's behind their faces and their work ethic and their acting, and into what they are living with, have been living with now for over two years.

Friday, March 15th.

To get a small sense of what people here have been living through, in terms of the day to day getting on with life. Last night, two air alerts; the first at 1:59am; immediately it became a heightened alert, more dangerous I think, but I'm not sure. It lasted a full hour. While waiting in the shelter, a man came in; so the two of us were there for the hour. I came back to my room, struggled to get back to sleep, then at six o'clock, another air alert and so back down to the shelter. This lasted only ten minutes, though it killed my sleep.

You never know, because any second everything can change, and you learn to accept this and move forward, or in the case of some people, you just ignore the alerts. I'm not in that position, and I don't think I will be during my stay here. I don't know enough and I will follow the directions of these alerts to a T.

Rehearsal this morning, it will be a straight 11am to 5pm. I don't have my Brutus all day; I don't have him again all of Sunday. I will need to jump around scenes, rehearsing out of order. I saw three of my actors in a play last night. It was very visual, the opposite of what we are trying to do.

Sunday, March 17th.

A couple of days ago Bohdan Benyuk, the artistic director, came up to me in the hallway, found a translator (he speaks no English), and said he "loved me" and that I was having "a huge influence on his theatre." I was of course moved by what he said; it implies that my actors are excited with what we're doing; focusing on the actor/character.

I had an interesting conversation with Arman at a late lunch after rehearsal. We talked about how I work as a director. Arman put this in a political context: Ukrainian theatre has had a long and deep connection to Russian theatre; in fact Theatre on Podil was a Russian-speaking theatre until a few years ago, before the war. Ukrainian theatre has its roots in Stanislavsky and character/actor-centric theatre. Theatre on Podil's founder, who died a few years ago, worked in this tradition. This theatre is still described on its website as a 'minimalist' theatre, meaning it's focused on character and story and not on visuals/sets. But the war has necessitated a split from all things Russian, and so Ukrainian theatre began to look in other directions for inspiration.

Much of European theatre has become director-driven and visually focused. German theatre, for example, is very physical with a lot of direct address, often with video and projections, often violent; and where the attempt is to discover a visual vocabulary. The plays I have seen so far in Kyiv seem to have the same dramatic ambition—the sets dominate, and seem more important to the director than the people. Even with *Oedipus Rex* the set held center stage and seemed to 'get in the way' of the acting. Arman talked about the need for Ukrainian theatre to find its own way, not by layering on outside influences; a way that is still connected to its roots. My work, he wondered, being not completely Stanislavsky, but its own kind of thing, and still very human-based, might have a special resonance in Ukraine right now.

Is this what Benyuk was saying to me?

WEEK THREE:

Monday, March 18th.
Day off:

Just back, moments ago, from an air-raid alert, down in the shelter; again I was the only one there. It didn't last long, about 12 or 14 minutes.

Today Oksana took me to Kyiv Lavra, an historic monastery; the oldest in Kyiv, begun around the 11th century. We took an Uber in the rain; we had an English-speaking guide, a man in his mid-forties. What I thought would be a tour of churches and church art, became, via our guide, a lesson in Ukraine's history. Ukraine as it is defined as being 'not-Russia'. Everything he pointed out—the art, the architecture—he described in terms of how Ukraine has always leaned toward the West; how it was, in fact, a European country with European aspirations. How its church art was different from Russian church art, and more connected to Roman Catholicism than to the Russian Orthodox Art. He pointed to an icon of Christ and explained how in Ukrainian church art Christ holds a book, and so their Christ was interested in teaching, learning; whereas in Russian church art, Christ held up his hands, to show his power. Our guide went on for well over an hour articulating such differences, while also recounting all the ways Russia had encroached upon Ukraine through the centuries and attempted to eliminate Ukraine as a country and its culture. In other words, he gave an historical context for everything that is going on now with this war, as seen through the history of church art.

The central church was a reconstruction; the original had been destroyed in World War II, "not by the invading Germans," our guide was quick to say, but "by the retreating Soviets in 1941."

One room of the church was devoted to remnants of churches destroyed in today's war by Russians.

This journey to a still functioning church and monastery, a center of religious life for centuries, became a fascinating afternoon of history, politics, and war. Oksana had hoped to have me experience Ukrainian art and culture, but today, like every day here, everything comes back to the war.

Oksana also wanted to teach me about Ukrainian theatre history and about a man, Les Kurbas, who in the early part of the 20th century was a major director in Ukraine—the father of modern Ukrainian theatre. He was often compared to Meyerhold and other major 20th-century directors. Kurbas created an entire movement of modern theatre in Ukraine, with theatres, theatre companies, schools, which eventually went against the grain of the Soviets. In the early 1930s he was arrested, sent to a work camp and then, in I think 1937, murdered.

I had never heard of him. Someone I need to learn more about. I am beginning to realize that there is a culture here, with its own rich and deep history, that for complicated and also obvious reasons has been hidden or repressed. Right now it's struggling to find its way into the awareness of the world. I think this is what Oksana is trying to get me to see.

Yesterday Arman mused about the Ukrainian language and the Russian language; how so many people around the theatre clearly have Russian as their first language, but for political or nationalistic reasons now speak only Ukrainian. He said that at certain points when they are frustrated and don't know what to say, they still resort to Russian. Things are not clear, clean, or simple in this world; it's a complicated place.

Almost 9pm:

I've been watching a movie on Netflix Ukrainian (with English subtitles) called *Kruty 1918*, made in 2018. A war movie, Ukrainians are fighting the Russians in 1918. A war film made in the midst of a war; so of course it's propaganda. But what's extraordinary is to be watching it while I'm here. I wonder if this is what it was like during World War II, watching films about heroes fighting the Germans or the Japanese. I felt I could understand what my parents were watching and feeling, and what movies were for them, in the 1940s.

Later that night:

The movie just ended with this line: "The price of freedom doesn't happen without bloodshed."

Tuesday, March 19th.

A lot of experiences today.

We couldn't rehearse in the theatre or the rehearsal room, because the whole building was taken over by the Minister of Culture for a series of conferences, including one led by the first lady, Mrs. Zelensky. We rehearsed in a space/room at a museum. We had a helpful discussion for the writer (me), as we all tried to figure out a rewrite for the end of the play; to not make it end on a note of agit-prop ("he must die"), but to keep the play domestic and human. I took notes and will work on this on my own.

Arman left today. He's been an incredible help. I'm hoping to get him back for the last two weeks of rehearsals.

With Arman and Larissa gone, I needed a new translator. I met with Yulia, an actress and an experienced translator. We had a good talk. She said something very interesting: that theatre in Ukraine has become extremely important since the war began. She doesn't remember a theatre ticket having so much currency as it does now, and that every theatre is full, everything is sold out, you can't get in, people are buying tickets months in advance. How did this happen and why? What is it about theatre right now? I wonder if it is people wanting to be together, watching, doing the same thing, and not being alone. Being able to express feelings in a group. I don't know, I will ask around.

After rehearsal, I met up with Oksana for a tour of the Bulgakov Museum, which is mostly closed now. The museum is across the street from the theatre. We had an hour-long-plus tour, with an English-speaking guide; interrupted by an air alert. I have promised myself and obviously Cindy that I will obey every air alert and find a shelter. We left and went to the shelter across the street in the theatre.

The plaque of Bulgakov on the front of the museum had been sprayed with red paint, like blood; his statue just outside is covered with sandbags so it won't be destroyed. Our guide explained that the museum has recently tried, or found the need, to change its focus. It had been a museum in praise of Mikhail Bulgakov, one of the great writers of the 20th century. This was his home where he grew up and the house he describes in minute detail in his novel *The White Guard*. But Bulgakov left Kyiv and went to Moscow where he began his writing career and now there are people in Ukraine who say he is a Russian writer. One of the first things our guide says to me, because I am American, is: "do I know about cancel culture?"

Bulgakov's plays are no longer performed in Ukraine; two had been in the repertory of Theatre on Podil across the street, and had been very popular. Our guide explained how in this time, during this war, many things are being eliminated, cultural elements that had been an integral part of Ukraine have been stripped away, because they are now seen as Russian.

The museum is now trying to tell the story of Ukraine as an independent country, Ukraine as separate, and to somehow connect this story to this house. So the Bulgakov Museum has for now become a museum of Kyiv during the time that Bulgakov lived here. A kind of hodgepodge, requiring a certain amount of juggling. At the moment the 'museum' feels neither one thing nor the other.

Wednesday, March 20th.

10:30am:

No rehearsal today until two this afternoon, because my Brutus had a show last night and needs some rest. So just three hours of rehearsal because of actors' conflicts. We'll work on Scene 6. We're making progress. I feel okay.

Yesterday, I walked back from the museum, where we rehearsed, to my hotel with one of my actresses. We passed the Opera (where the ballet also performs), a beautiful building. She explained how Russia had always poached the best students from Kyiv's ballet and drama schools; the moment they were trained they were sent to Moscow or St. Petersburg.

12:30pm:

I am in the hotel shelter. We just had an air alert. And I am down here, as almost always, by myself. I notice on my phone app that the Kyiv area seems to be targeted, so this might be a longer wait than normal. We'll see. I am here with my computer. I supposedly have rehearsal in an hour and a half, so hopefully this is all concluded by then.

I was wrong; it lasted only about 20 minutes. It's about 1pm; I am heading off to rehearsal.

6:45pm:

An unsatisfying rehearsal.

I had moved the start of rehearsal from 11am to 2pm at my Brutus' request, because he had had a show last night. He then forgot this and arrived at 11am, and so had to sit around for three hours. By the time we began, he was already tired. Yulia, our new translator, seems very good, but having any new person in the room creates a little unease. Arman with his good energy wasn't there. My assigned assistant sat in for a while; but his energy is mostly in other directions; he is also busy directing a play. My Cicero seemed distracted, he has a show tonight. We worked until 5pm and his show is at 6pm, so maybe his mind was there. My Porcia also seemed in another place. She speaks English and I wondered if having someone else doing the translating was disconcerting.

We started on Scene 6, maybe the most complicated scene in the play. We ended up just talking it through for three hours. I made a few small changes and cuts, but we never got it on its feet. Tomorrow we move onto Scene 7. If we have time we may go back and try to put Scene 6 on its feet. We are now moving slowly. Also a rainy day. Goodnight.

Thursday, March 21st.

5:19am:

I have now been in the shelter for hours. "Increased air alert in your air, proceed to the nearest shelter."

6:18am:

I have the television on, President Zelensky is speaking live, though of course in Ukrainian.

The headline in the *Kyiv Independent* is:

UPDATE: Russia launches mass missile attack on Kyiv, injuring 8.

Russian forces launched a missile attack on Kyiv early in the morning of March 21, causing multiple explosions throughout the city and wounding at least four people.

According to Kyiv Mayor Vitalii Klitschko, at least eight residents were injured in the attack. They all received medical treatment and none of the victims has required hospitalization.

Serhiy Popko, head of the Kyiv City Military Administration, said one of the victims was a child.

The attack damaged apartment buildings, a kindergarten, a business, infrastructure, and vehicles. Emergency services are working at the attack sites and the full extent of the damage is being investigated amid ongoing attacks.

> *The Air Force reported that Russian forces launched Kinzhal ballistic missiles at Kyiv overnight. The military also warned of missile threats throughout the country.*
>
> *Multiple explosions were heard in Kyiv early in the morning of March 21 amid threats of a massive Russian missile attack, according to reports from city and military authorities.*
>
> *A series of explosions occurred in the capital around 5am, Klitschko said.* Kyiv Independent *correspondents reported hearing over a dozen in the city.*
>
> *Falling rock fragments in the Podilskyi district caused a fire to break out at a transformer substation and at a two-story non-residential building, Klitschko reported.*
>
> *The roof of a residential building in the Podilskyi district is also on fire.*
>
> *In the Svyatoshynsky district, the attack damaged a kindergarten and two nine-story apartment buildings.*
>
> *A residential building in the Shevchenkivskyi district was also hit, Klitschko said. Residents are being evacuated from the burning building. Cars are on fire in the area and firefighters have been dispatched to the scene.*

I have just gotten out of the shelter after over three hours. Went in at 3:21am. The threat was increased at 4:17am. I was alone until about then, when others started to come in, eventually we were 14 people including two little dogs. That's everyone in the hotel. The young woman who manages the front desk was in charge; she had corralled everybody. She told me she had gotten worried when she heard the sound of drones very near, in this district. She said they sounded like scooters, and were quite close.

From the shelter I could hear explosions. I follow along on a Telegram chat: a car burning, rocket fragments having fallen on Podil around 5:20am. Around 5:40am a transformer substation in Podil was hit by rocket debris and by rocket fire. By 5:43am, the roof of a residential building was on fire in Podil. No victims needing hospitalization so far.

It was interesting to note the different groups coming into the shelter; clearly not wanting to be there, tired. I had a chat with the front desk woman, who has always been nice to me; she said she usually isn't scared when she's at home with her family, but here, she had the responsibility of finding everybody and bringing them down into the shelter. This was only the second time in the two years of war when the hotel made everybody come down into the shelter.

I've been up for the past three plus hours, I will try and get to sleep. I also want to take a hot shower, as it is cold down there, and last night for some reason there was no water. I'll stop this now and get on with my day.

[An email from a friend, an actress who had been in my play in Paris:

Dearest Richard,

Everything is OK? I just heard news about some attacks this morning in Kiev but don't know where ?
Are your actors, family, and friends all OK?
Take care
Love
S

Dear S,

I am fine; safe and sound. It was an eventful night; when the alert sounded I went to the shelter—as I have now done many, many times; and as usual I was the only person there for the first hour. Then a more critical alert sounded, and the rest of the hotel (about 9 or 10 people and 2 dogs) joined for the next 2½ hours.
I could hear explosions from the shelter—the missile defense system shooting down the rockets—but always felt totally safe.

So an adventure. And a loss of sleep for me and my actors, so we shortened rehearsal yesterday.

At the moment, as I write, it is 5 in the morning and I am back in the shelter; the air-raid alert having sounded a half-hour ago. It is comfortable here—water, blankets, magazines, and internet. No one has joined me so I suspect nothing is happening, at least in terms of Kyiv. But I wait for the 'all-clear'.

My actors are very good; and I am really enjoying myself. Though I think of all of you!!!! And miss you.

Thank you for checking in. Check in again any time.

I send my love from this very beautiful city.

xx]

Friday, March 22nd.
7:06am:

Just emerged from the shelter, I have been there for a little over two and a half hours. In there by myself for a while, then after the alert was heightened, three people came in, a couple and an older man who seems to speak English. After about an hour the couple left; after another 20 minutes, the man left, so I was again down there by myself waiting until the all-clear, the announcement, "May the Force Be With You."

I followed along on Telegram: various parts of the country were being attacked, Kharkiv especially. It seems that they lost all power. There seems to be an effort to go after Western Ukraine as well, Lviv, and also Zhevoricha. I'll know more when I hear more reports today.

We will rehearse at 11am. I am trying to decide whether to go back to bed for a while, or just stay up, take a shower, shave, and at 8 o'clock go have breakfast (this is when the hotel restaurant opens). I think we'll once again make it a short day, work 11am to 4pm, no evening rehearsal. I'm probably not the only one who lost sleep tonight. So, on to Scene 7 and Scene 8 with new rewrites. Our new translator Yulia is making the translation of these rewrites for Scene 8.

5pm:

I decided, on a trial basis, to permanently shorten rehearsal to 11 to 4 with a half-an-hour break, instead of 11am—3pm and 4pm—7pm. I need to give everyone time to breathe and to rest; to begin to focus on learning lines. I'll see how this goes; we're working hard, and made a rough draft of staging Scenes 7 and 8. Tomorrow I will work on Scene 4 and hopefully review Scenes 1 through 3. Then we'll see where we are. People are tired because of shows, tired because of air raids; I think this is the right thing to do.

Various conversations today. I was talking to my Cicero without a translator, so through gestures and his little bits of English and whatnot. He tells me about the problem he has with his knees. When this war started he joined the civil defense force and so had to stay up all night, patrolling. He's 65 years old. He wonders if that is why his knees hurt. Or if it is just the atmosphere, and by 'atmosphere' I am pretty sure he means 'the tension, the anxiety' that is in the air.

While we talked a man passed us in the hallway and said hello. He is a director of another show. After he had passed, my Cicero explained that the man's brother was killed last year in the war, leaving three small children. And he hadn't gotten over this. My Cicero held his hand to his heart.

After rehearsal I met with the company manager to work out my rehearsal schedule and the various conflicts; she told me that her 90-year-old mother is in intensive care in the hospital, but fortunately she is in a 'modern' hospital, and one not yet overcrowded with wounded soldiers.

I read this in today's *Kyiv Independent:*

Russia launched another large-scale drone and missile attack against Ukrainian cities overnight on March 22. Regional authorities said that there were at least five killed and 31 injured among the casualties reported so far.

"The enemy launched one of the largest attacks on the Ukrainian energy sector in recent weeks," Energy Minister Herman Halushchenk wrote on Facebook.

"The goal is not just to damage it, but, just like last year, to cause a large-scale disruption in the country's energy system."

"Russia launched 60 Shahed-type drones and almost 90 missiles of various types against Ukraine in the overnight strike," President Volodymyr Zelensky said.

"There are no delays in Russian missiles like there are in assistance to our country," Zelensky wrote on Telegram.

Later that night:

Before I go to bed, I have learned to set out a pair of socks, my pants, a shirt, get my knapsack ready and my shoes in a place where I can easily find them, so that I can get dressed quickly in time to go to the shelter. So I've got sort of a 'shelter plan' or 'dress plan' in place, after a number of nights being woken up.

Saturday, March 23rd.
6:50am:

Last night in Moscow: a shooting at a concert; untold people killed and wounded. ISIS claimed responsibility. The US says there is no indication whatsoever of Ukraine's involvement, which Russia is claiming. Ukraine, however, is implying that "*this is a deliberate provocation by Putin's Special Services about which the international community warned. The public execution of people in Moscow should be understood as Putin's threat of an even greater escalation and expansion of war. The US had warned that extremists had planned to attack a large gathering, however the unimpeded movement of a group of militants through the center of Moscow as well as a lot of other indisputable evidence indicates that the shooting in the Concert Hall was organized by the Russian Special Services.*" (*Kyiv Independent*)

In 1999, shortly after Putin became President, a series of bombings rocked Russia and Chechen separatists were blamed. It has since been widely speculated that Russia's security organization, the FSB, orchestrated these bombings to boost Putin's popularity.

Just hours after the attacks last night, former Russian president Medvedev warned of retaliation against Ukraine. "Death for death," he said.

I woke up in the middle of the night, I had gotten a WhatsApp text from Ariane Mnouchkine in Paris, the artistic director and founder of Théâtre du Soleil, where I have just been working:

Dear Richard,
I would like to speak to you about what just happened in Moscow. If you read me now call me.
If not, let's speak tomorrow morning.
Love
Ariane

I know what she wants to talk about. She is worried about me, and that the bombing in Moscow is a repeat of what happened with Chechnya. The next few days will be interesting, as we see how this plays out, what actually is going on and what has really happened.

I will soon head to rehearsal, which is at 11am; I will be there by 10am to set up the furniture. We'll go back and do the opening of the play plus a review and reworking of Scene 4. All goes forward with rehearsal. All is good. Glory to Ukraine.

I wrote to Ariane:

Just got up and got your message. This morning I have rehearsal beginning at 10am your time, a break around 1pm (noon your time) when I could call you, we break at 3pm your time and I am free and around after that. Much love,

xx

Dear Richard,

My fears are now legitimated by Putin's recent 'diagnosis' of the Moscow attack. I just want to know if the US Embassy is conscious of you being present in Kyiv? I really think you must consider the situation very carefully and be aware of the risks you are willing to take or not.

I am really concerned and very anxious about what could happen to Ukraine any day now. And consequently to you, my friend.

Let me know what your working companions are saying.
Lots of Love
Ariane

Dear Ariane,

Yes, I have been watching this closely. I registered with the Embassy before arriving; so they should know. I am now in the hotel shelter in an air alert—but these are common as you know, pretty much at least once a day. I am careful, obey every warning. One thought of course is that he is using the Moscow attack as an excuse to prepare for a greater mobilization. He's been eyeing the need for this for some time; and now he can give an excuse that doesn't relate to the failure of his military campaign. If this is the case, Ukraine won't face the full force of this until early summer, I think.

But that is only one theory. My working companions live their lives. I do not get any sense of extra anxiety, that is, any more concern than they already have and have had for two years. In any event, I will be vigilant. And I will keep you informed of any change that I see from here. As you know Kyiv is a well-protected city; though nothing can be totally protected given everything. Let's see. There is probably no one in the world who I know, who would understand better than you—that being here, making theatre, at this time, is an extraordinary gift to me. I send my love. xx

*I send you mine, my dear friend. Work well.
Love and lots of it.
Ariane*

President Zelensky after the Moscow Terror attack:

760 days of Russia's full-scale war against Ukraine. More than two years of clear evidence of what Putin's system is bringing to the world. Ruins instead of cities and villages. Death and pain, not life. Terror instead of international law. Ukrainians are bravely defending their homeland and will continue to do so. I am grateful to everyone around the world who supports our country and people. I am grateful to everyone who calls a spade a spade and refuses to let Russia deceive the world through propaganda and blackmail. Russia must lose this war. This is the only way to reliably protect human lives. Air defense, long-range weapons, artillery, sanctions, the confiscation of Russian assets, and support for our country all bring the restoration of a fair peace and normal life closer.

Almost 7:30pm:

Had almost a five-hour rehearsal today.

One thing that is so unique (I hear myself laugh on the recording as I transcribe this) about this experience, is having picked out the furniture for my play from the storage—large table, small table, stool, chairs, and rugs, it all suddenly disappears before rehearsal today. I'm told that this furniture, like my actors, is also in other plays! No one told me this and so I watch two men come in and take it all away. I've been able to hold onto most of the chairs. At one point in rehearsal we had seat cushions, but they have gone too. We don't seem to have the same props from one rehearsal to the next. It's an adventure.

I'm in a theatre that does over 40 shows in rep, and without much storage space so props, furniture are constantly recycled. Someone surely has a list of all the pieces that are needed for each show. Or maybe it is just in someone's mind?

I stopped rehearsal at one point today because I felt that a couple of the actors were going off on a wrong track, heavily 'acting' when that is the exact opposite of what I am after. I sat everyone down and went back to explaining what I am trying to do, which is to create human conversations, as close to real-life human conversation as possible, and do this in front of an audience, while not trying to show the audience anything, not trying to do anything for them, but to just be. To let the audience have that sort of experience; something very, very human. And let them experience these characters working through the complexity of their issues and their problems. I think it was a good talk, I think we gained something from it. But I think we're going to have to have this talk again and again.

Putin has gone on TV to say that he thinks Ukraine somehow carried a responsibility for the terrorist attack in Moscow. He claims the captured terrorists were on their way to Ukraine. Maybe he is trying to create a situation where he can call up for soldiers, which is what he needs to do, or maybe he is going to expand the attacks on Ukraine. We'll find out.

Sunday, March 24th.

6am:

Just left the shelter, where I was for about two and a half hours. Kyiv was again attacked by missiles. From the shelter I heard two explosions; someone in the shelter said there were actually three. I heard two.

I was the first person in there, then a woman came in, and eventually another four people found their way there, including the same woman from the front desk.

I spent my time reading a draft of the program notes for a play of mine soon opening in London; and sent my corrections.

I think it's time to go back to bed for a little while. We have rehearsal in a few hours.

Later in the morning:

As I mentioned, yesterday at rehearsal after a quick run of part of a scene I stopped everything, brought everyone to the table and tried to explain again what I'm trying to do, what my aesthetic is, how they, my actors, need to put aside what they are used to. How we need to forge a new, different, way of acting on stage together. One where the actors really talk and really listen to each other, where they need to have these conversations; where they 'show' nothing to the audience and do not 'do' anything for them. Or as Harley Granville Barker, the early 20th-century playwright/director and a thinker I much admire, would say, "just be."

It was a good thing to do; because one actress had been sort of sucking the energy out of the room, even being a bit rude, I thought, which is a very rare occurrence in my rehearsals. I'm not sure where this was coming from, but I thought she was showing me she wasn't understanding or maybe approving of the way we were working. The pause was good and helpful; she is very smart and talented. I do think she began to understand and even got excited. She wanted to keep working on her scene, but I had to move on.

I explained that what I was trying to do was not the 'American' way of acting, I wasn't bringing something from America; this was simply something personal. I tried to give a history of my own work, or the last 25 years since I became a director of my own plays. I described how I had been encouraged to tour this aesthetic, how my work had been discovered by important directors like Ariane Mnouchkine, Peter Brook, Thomas Ostermeier. My actors seemed intrigued—intrigued is too modest a word—I think they were excited and certainly my Cicero is thrilled with my approach. I felt the same with the others. We'll see.

Yesterday also was frustrating because the actors started telling me about more conflicts they had with rehearsals; how they couldn't come this day or that. I had sat for hours with the company manager, who is in charge of managing all conflicts, and so I thought my schedule was set. I was taken aback, feeling—"am I being used?" "Am I being taken advantage of?"

After rehearsal, my Syrus came up to me and said, "I don't know if you know, but I need to have three days off this week." I was skeptical, and then he explained that his son is in the military and is going to the front lines, but before he does, he is getting married. My Syrus needs these days to prepare his son's wedding before going to war.

Later that day:

This on Telegram, from *The Times of Ukraine* chat group:

May the day be peaceful, beautiful, sunny in Ukraine. Gather friends you haven't seen for a long time. And enjoy your Sunday. Let's resist.

About 5:30pm:

Finished rehearsal; even though we were all tired with the air alerts having kept us up, it was a good day. We started with the prologue, and then did Scene 1; second half of Scene 2 and all of Scene 3. A good way to end the week.

Leaving the rehearsal room, I was stopped by the company manager, who runs and organizes the schedule for the entire theatre and for the actors. She asked about my schedule for the week and when I would need the rehearsal room. I said I am now working 11am to 4pm. This pleased her no end, because, she explained, the rehearsal room was now needed from 5pm during the week. Two of the company's actors have been called up for military service and, I think she said, headed to the front. The roles they played now need to be recast with other actors, and re-rehearsed. This was why the rehearsal room is now needed.

Later:

At rehearsal today, one of my actors told me that my talk about what I am trying to do was important and how afterwards the actors were indeed excited, spoke about this, and how they now understood what I was after.

Tomorrow is a day off.

WEEK FOUR:

Monday, March 25th.
7:30am:

My day off; I have nothing scheduled, no place I have to go or have to be. I will go to the bank, get my laundry done, do some grocery shopping for snacks, maybe take a stroll, see a little more of Kyiv—that which I can do by foot.

I want to do some work, and continue to keep typing up this diary; work out a schedule for the week and maybe beyond that. It's complicated, especially without having a stage manager right now, as she is in the hospital. The process is tricky, not just how to schedule, but also how to let people know the schedule. Anyway, all that will work out. I want to sort out sound cues throughout the show and be in touch with the sound designer, so we can begin to use cues in rehearsal.

A good night's sleep, no air alerts, no air raids. A quiet night.

I want to write down one thought I had sitting in the shelter the other night: I was looking around and thinking about what I should write about this in my diary. I looked at the few people who were also there, people who are Ukrainian, people who cannot leave, and I felt guilty. What I'm writing about—they are living. Of course I'm living in it too, but for a brief time. They are looking down the road, thinking—"what is my life going to be, what is my country going to be—what is the future?"

I read this in the *Kyiv Independent*:

"Russia launched close to 190 missiles, 140 Shahed drones, and 700 aerial bombs at Ukraine over the last week," President Volodymyr Zelensky said in his evening address on March 24.

More than 200,000 homes remain without stable power in the city of Kharkiv and one district in Kharkiv Oblast, Zelenksy said.

Russian forces targeted over 130 energy infrastructure facilities on March 21-22 and critically damaged one of the stations of the Dnipro Hydroelectric Power Plant, Ukraine's largest hydroelectric station.

The Institute for the Study of War (ISW) noted on March 22 that Russia hopes to collapse Ukraine's energy grid as the country struggles with air defense shortages.

Around 10:30am:

I'm on a WhatsApp call with a friend in Copenhagen when I suddenly hear the air-raid sirens go off outside. My phone, however, does not sound an alarm, so for a moment I'm confused. I tell my friend I better go, but even before I can hang up, I hear explosions quite nearby, two, three, four, I can't quite tell. I hang up and I hurry down to the shelter—the first time I really rush. I have grabbed the charger for my computer, my computer, and my bag. Rushing, I bump my head against the opened bathroom door. I hurry down where soon there are three, four, five other people joining me.

I learn from Telegram that there were explosions in the center of Kyiv, not that far from me.

Within half an hour there is an all-clear. Not quite sure why my phone didn't send an alarm; that was a new thing. And now I am back at my desk.

I read in the *Kyiv Independent*:

Russia launches another missile attack on Kyiv, at least 2 injured.

A series of explosions rocked Kyiv on March 25 as Russia launched yet another missile attack on Ukraine's capital.

Kyiv Independent correspondents in the capital heard at least four loud explosions just seconds after air-raid sirens sounded at around 10:30am local time and saw smoke rising from the left bank of the city.

In a post on Telegram, Kyiv's military administration urged residents to take shelter "urgently."

The building hit was the Kyiv State Academy of Decorative and Applied Arts, and the academy's gym and concert hall were destroyed, according to a Kyiv Independent reporter on the ground, citing the institution's employees. The Culture Ministry confirmed the academy was struck, adding that an employee was wounded.

An apartment building in Kyiv's Pecherskyi district was damaged in Russia's morning missile strike against Kyiv.

Debris from intercepted missiles damaged two houses in the Solomianskyi district and a house in the Darnytskyi district, where the attack also caused a fire in a non-residential building, according to the city authorities.

As of 3:30pm local time, the number of victims in Kyiv's Pecherskiy district rose to 10.

The all-clear siren sounded in Kyiv just after 11:00am.

Later in the morning following the attack, Air Force Commander Mykola Oleschuk said Russia had launched two ballistic missiles from occupied Crimea and that both had been intercepted by the air defenses.

United States Ambassador to Ukraine, Bridget Brink, said: "Again this morning Russia is attacking Ukraine with hypersonic missiles. Loud explosions in Kyiv."

Later that morning:

I just watched a video on Telegram of the air raid earlier this morning, showing small children running for cover and screaming while explosions are heard. Every time there is an explosion the children scream. The translation is "children run to the shelter of a kindergarten, while air alarms and explosions sound in Kyiv." This happened very close to here, right now, in March, 2024.

Later in the morning:

One of my actors just wrote to me on Telegram, "it has been a long time since we've had an alarm and then at once rockets. They say they were super-fast rockets. I hope you are safe and not scared."

7pm:

There was another air alert a couple of hours ago. I went down to the shelter, where I was joined by a young Ukrainian woman. I'd seen her before on a few occasions in the shelter over the last two or three days. She and I were the only two people there. We smiled at each other and said hello.

And today we talked.

She lives in the Netherlands, is here visiting friends and family, and is staying at this hotel because it has a shelter. Her husband's and her family don't go to shelters anymore. She is probably heading back to the Netherlands tomorrow or the next day. We talked tonight about the alert this morning and how it just 'suddenly' happened. The air raid sirens went on and within seconds, there were the explosions. She said she was in a taxi on the bridge over the Dnipro, on her way to the left bank, where most of the explosions were happening at the time. She could see puffs of smoke coming up; the taxi stopped on the bridge and a military vehicle passed, unsheathing a gun which began shooting into the sky. As all this was happening, seeing her concern, the taxi driver turned around and said, "don't worry, dear, you're with me."

We talked about many things; she's been in the Netherlands for six years; I think she has some complex feelings coming back to Kyiv. She had made her decision to leave long ago, and then the war happened, and now she feels… what? She sees people living, trying to live the life they had, but at the same time knowing that everything is changing, that there is no certainty about any future. And how there is anxiety in their faces, all the time. She says the city feels very different than the one she left, the people seem different. But then again, she said there's also a feeling that they want to live, that they are going to live and make the most of their lives, moment to moment. So, she said, there is that as well.

For some reason she thought I was a journalist. When I told her I was a playwright she became very interested; and I think, pleased. She smiled and said that what I'm doing is really important right now. Art is important right now.

I think she's a businesswoman, she used to work for eBay when it was in Kyiv and now works for some other business in the Netherlands. So I met a friend! Met a colleague, a cohort, to share the shelter with; too bad she leaves the next day.

Tuesday, March 26th.
About 6:30am:

I woke up to a Telegram message saying that my Brutus is ill, has a fever, headache. So that changes today's rehearsal, because today was built around him.

I also woke up thinking about something the young woman in the shelter told me yesterday: how the people in the Netherlands have no idea that such a thing as this war could ever happen to them. It is simply inconceivable to them. There are no shelters there; no place to hide, not even forests. Yet they are so close to here. In miles. In distance.

5:25pm:
After rehearsal.

No Brutus because he is sick. He will probably still be sick tomorrow too. And because the day had been planned around all of his scenes, it was complicated. We tried working on two scenes just with my Cassius—then also with Cicero when he was free at 2pm. I had a long conversation with my Cassius. He teaches at three different schools and acts with another theatre as well. He and Yulia, my translator, talked about the state of theatre in Ukraine. They didn't know much about American theatre but were curious. We shared tales or, mostly, frustrations about our various theatres.

Our stage manager is back; she got a plate removed from her ankle. She was in the hospital for a few days. I asked her what had happened: last year during a blackout because of a power outage, she was walking her dog, tripped, and severely broke her ankle. She said that the Russians had caused this, because the blackout was due to their bombing a power station.

My Cicero asked me about yesterday, when the siren went off and the bombing started immediately. I told him I heard it, how it felt nearby. He said he felt it too, and his dog was very scared. He asked how Cindy was doing with my being here, and was she scared. I said, she is worried of course, but strong, and she's been supportive. He asked if I would thank her for all of them for my being here.

Today I will talk to Cindy on WhatsApp, as I do every night, and I will tell her that. She'll be pleased.

So a simple day so far, we'll see what the night brings.

About 8:40pm:

We just had another air alert. I went down to the shelter and the young Ukrainian woman, my 'shelter-mate' hadn't left yet, she was there. She'd beaten me. We had a nice long chat; she's full of a lot of anxieties, and yet very funny too. As we were leaving, she said how great it's been to have me to talk to. I was like 'the taxi driver' from her story the other day. That made me laugh. She definitely leaves for home tomorrow.

Wednesday, March 27th.
Morning:

No air alerts, so a solid night's sleep. Because I prepare for the alerts by going to bed quite early, thinking I could easily be woken up at any hour, it means, on a night with no air alerts, I wake up very early.

I woke up thinking about the conversation with my Cassius yesterday; it took me a while to unpack what he was saying. He talked about the theatre, and having mentors—not as teachers but as examples—those theatre artists who believed in theatre, and whose careers a young actor could try and emulate. He said that the actors who were in their twenties in the 1980s did have mentors, examples of theatre artists in the Soviet Union to look up to. Actors who saw themselves first as artists and who believed in the value and significance of theatre as an art. Then in the 1990s, these young actors, with the collapse of the Soviet Union, found the theatre in chaos; and their lives became about survival, how to make money, how to make a living from acting. These are now the older actors of today and they have retained that mindset—the need to make money, to take this job or that job, how to get this job or that job. And the notion that theatre is an art has been nearly forgotten or lost. These are now the 'mentors' of today's younger actors like my Cassius, who is in his thirties.

So a young actor today feels adrift, without anything or anyone to follow, or look up to; without a solid basis on which to build a career as an artist and not just as a working actor.

A peek into another's theatre; as I have stared into mine, finding it unsatisfying, compromised, lost.

On Monday, just before the air alert and the explosions that surprised me, I was WhatsApping with my actor friend in Copenhagen. He too was sharing his disappointment with Danish theatre; how he finds it hard to be an artist in that world. Perhaps this is how it's always been, or perhaps it reflects something else, something larger about how society, culture, theatre is evolving or already has evolved.

About 3:30pm:

When I got to the rehearsal room this morning I learned my Brutus will be out sick for the rest of the week, on doctor's orders. I am glad he is resting and taking care of himself.

My Cicero arrived wearing a mask, saying he too was not well; with aches all over and a sore throat. I sent him home.

But not before he told me about the show he did last night with Bohdan Benyuk. At the curtain call Benyuk gave a speech, as is the custom here now. It is usually about the war, but this time he talked about me, telling the audience I was here, directing my play, how special this was, and repeating what I had told him, how proud I said I was to be here at this time.

My Servilia arrived late because of traffic.

My Cassius and Yulia arrived. But there was little I could rehearse.

My Syrus' son is getting married before going to war, so my Syrus is at home.

My Porcia is filming in Odesa.

I have only two of my actors, and these two characters never have a scene together. I suggest we spend time learning lines. I have no idea what I can rehearse, without a Brutus and Cicero for the rest of the week.

Rehearsal today became a conversation with my Cassius, Yulia, and my Servilia about Ukrainian theatre. My Cassius invited me to come and speak to his students next week, which I said I would be happy to do. We talked a little about my play; mostly about the style that I work in, how they must keep it together in the future when I am not around; that is, how to keep the relationships going when you haven't played the play for over a month. Because Theatre on Podil plays in repertory, my play will only be performed once or twice a month at most. I didn't have answers because I've never worked this way before. So I said we'll see. One can always film a show and send it to me and I can send back notes.

I've decided to do as many invited dress rehearsals as possible, maybe as many as seven, so that the actors can get into a groove before the press performance which actually is the first public performance. The second and third performances are the opening. So I want to give them a little bit of a 'run'. We'll see if I am being too optimistic.

I will now finish up my tour of the Bulgakov home which was interrupted by the air raid.

Then I go off with Oksana to see a concert at the Philharmonic.

A little while later:

As I walked out of the theatre this afternoon, in front of me were two men, one a soldier in camouflage uniform, walking on a wounded leg, with a crutch.

About 6:40pm:

I just completed my tour at the Bulgakov Museum. The tour guide wanted to film me reading a passage from Bulgakov's *The Theatrical Novel*, and she also asked me to sign a book. She took my photo next to the lamp with the green shade which was Bulgakov's; this lamp famously figures in *The Master and Margarita*.

Our guide seemed in pain talking about the criticism this museum has received, and about the attacks on Bulgakov for being anti-Ukraine and pro-Russian empire. She struggled to describe how the museum's focus is no longer on the writer, but on the time when he lived here in Kyiv, a time when Ukraine had a brief moment of independence from Russia.

An independent Ukraine separate from Russia: this is the theme repeated over and over in vastly different contexts. I feel I am watching a country be born.

This letter by Bulgakov to a sister is in the museum:

"I've been sleeping now and dreaming about Kiev, dear, familiar faces, somebody playing the piano... Will the good old times be ever back again? The present is so repellent that to live overlooking it... without seeing or hearing! Recently when travelling to Moscow and Saratov I got to see everything with my own eyes, and I'd like to see no more of it. I saw grey crowds breaking train windows with giggling and sickening swearing, I saw beating people. I saw destroyed and burnt buildings in Moscow... dull and brutal faces... I saw crowds attacking doors of seized and locked banks, hungry queues near shops, persecuted and miserable officers, I saw newspapers reporting on blood flowing in the south, west, and east, and jails. I saw everything first hand, and ultimately realized what happened.... New Year's coming. Big kisses. Your brother Mikhail."

11pm:

I am back from the shelter. I had finished talking with Cindy, and the alert went off. And with my young shelter mate gone, I was again there by myself. I was there for about 40 minutes. This after a beautiful evening; Oksana had taken me to hear the Ukrainian National Orchestra, in a gorgeous hall in Kyiv, to hear Mozart's clarinet concerto and a symphony by Elgar. Fantastic acoustics, extraordinary orchestra, a beautiful night.

> I read this in *Times of Ukraine* Telegram chat:
>
> *Air alarms in Kyiv, the northern and central regions of Ukraine are becoming more frequent due to the accumulated Zircon missiles in the occupied Crimea... The enemy has collected at least several dozen such missiles on the peninsula and the targeted terror with an emphasis on the capital can continue.*

Thursday, March 28th.
About 9:45am:

I will go to rehearsal pretty soon. I'm not sure what to do... I've called a rehearsal for work on learning lines. I have just learned my Porcia is also sick; that my Cicero remains sick but hopes to be back tomorrow. My Servilia is excused because her husband is having his 50th birthday party today and she needs to prepare. Syrus' son gets married today before going off to the front. Brutus remains ill. That leaves Cassius as the only available actor.

It will be one of those days.

I wrote to Oksana that we don't need a director but a doctor.

A little before 4pm:

We finished rehearsal early. I just had my Cassius all day, Yulia translating. And it was a useful session. I think we made progress figuring out a couple of tricky scenes with Cassius. I'm surprised we got so much work done with just one actor.

I met two young, college-age women who will begin to work as my translators next week, overlapping with Yulia for a week, before she has to go away for a while. They are both young acting students, both speak English. I hope this works out; it will certainly be a good experience for them. I tried to summarize for them the background of the play and how I work.

They both said that theatre has become much more important since the war. This must be the third or fourth time someone has said this to me, but these young women said it had become much more important for young people like themselves. Before the war theatre was for older people, or for 'grown ups' as they called them (us), but now it's young people who are going to the theatre.

Benyuk came by and asked me to come and speak to his students; it turns out these are the same students as my Cassius', at the same school.

Oksana has begun arranging a workshop for me with students and professionals in the theatre.

Yulia, my translator, said something that struck me and moved me. We had an air alert in the middle of the day, so we continued to work in the theatre lobby/shelter. My Cassius liked working down there, around people talking, so we stayed there for the rest of the day, even after the alert was over. As we were leaving, Yulia said to me, "for me there have been very few moments of happiness in the last two years, and working today in the lobby with you," she said, "was one of them."

Afternoon:

Yulia explained how Russia puts planes in the air not to launch missiles, but rather because they know that the planes will cause an air alert, which means public transportation stops. The point then is to terrorize and exhaust the Ukrainian population, but Ukrainians have gotten so used to this they ignore the alerts. This is why I'm often the only one in the shelter. Sometimes these flights last for hours; they circle around, refuel in the air, just to keep the alerts alive.

Friday, March 29th.
3:58am:

I am alone in the shelter for the second time tonight. Something feels odd, like something unusual is going on. First alert was at 2:04am, waking me out of a dream. It lasted more than a half an hour. When it ended, I went back to my room and as I struggled to get back to sleep, the second alert came. Two, back-to-back: this hasn't happened before.

4:39am:

Increased air alert. Still in the shelter. Still alone. I'll see if others join.

6:12am:

Alert is over. I am back to my room and will try and get a little sleep. It's been a long night in the shelter. From what I read on Telegram Kyiv itself was not targeted; but there seem to have been a great number of attacks around the country, especially in the west around Lviv, which has lost power. I'm sure I'll learn more later this morning. Now to bed for at least an hour.

9:30pm:

I saw Theatre on Podil's production of Kafka's *The Trial* this evening. A young woman played Josef K; I gather she is a dancer, and she was fantastic. She was like a female Chaplin. My Cassius was in it and very good. Visually beautiful. But the young Josef K was something special.

Hopefully I will get through the whole night tonight, because I need the sleep. I had dinner, potato pancakes, at the hotel, where the waiters of course know me by now. When I asked for my bill, the waiter said there's a problem. "Your bill comes to 666 hryvnias." He said we can't accept that. Obviously some superstition, so I had to buy another glass of wine, to avoid the number 666. [I learned this relates to the 6th day that God created the world, but before he'd blessed it on the 7th; so this number, 666, is attached to Satan.]

Saturday, March 30.
Around 6pm:

Took a long walk after rehearsal; a beautiful day; almost 70 degrees. Walked down the hill to the Ferris Wheel, went to the bank, then sat outside. Rehearsal good, interrupted by one air raid but we continued to work in the lobby.

I received an email from the US Embassy, warning that hypersonic missiles could be part of Russia's arsenal now and they take only seconds to arrive, so be on the lookout, whatever that means.

> ***Security Alert***: *U.S. Embassy Kyiv, Ukraine (March 30, 2024)*
> ***Location***: *Ukraine (countrywide)*
> ***Event***: *Recent Russian air attacks across Ukraine, including daytime attacks with surface-to-surface hypersonic missiles, underscore the potential for sudden shifts in Russian tactics and the capability of some Russian weapon systems to reach Ukrainian cities only a few minutes following launch. We remind all U.S. citizens to be vigilant of their personal safety and to take immediate shelter upon hearing an air alert or explosion.*

I shared this with the actors, they all knew it. President Zelensky had said the exact same thing several days ago. When I read it to them, they laughed, snorted, and said, "we've been doing this for two years." As if to say: what kind of advice is the American Embassy going to give us? I think I will hold back on sharing that kind of advice in the future.

I spent the morning writing notes for the program; I want to make clear who the characters are, their relationships with each other; after all it's a family play. I wrote out a timeline of the history, as briefly as possible and only what is necessary for the play. And at Oksana's suggestion, I wrote this short statement as to why I am here, and how I got to Kyiv. I sent it to Oksana and she thinks it's fine.

HOW I GOT HERE

I wrote Conversations in Tusculum *several years ago, and directed its premiere in 2008 at the Public Theater in New York City. There was something about that time in the U.S. that made me want to explore one of the most famous dictators in history and his sudden and surprising demise. I found myself drawn not to the plotting of the assassination, but rather to how very smart, 'decent' people, could believe in their ability to handle and control this dictator. So I set my play, not around the famous 'event', but during the summer before, as those who eventually would become assassins seek reasonable solutions to the problem of a dictator like Caesar, all the time hoping that they will have an effect. I felt these were interesting, complex characters; confused, lost, angry, and eventually self-questioning, even self-loathing.*

I did not think about this play for a long time. Then when Ukraine was again invaded in February 2022, my mind wandered back to those characters who did not see what was coming, who thought they could handle 'Caesar.' I started to think that the play was worth doing again. A friend in Paris agreed with me, she showed the play to a Ukrainian actor, who then showed it to Bohdan Benyuk, the artistic director of Theatre on Podil. We soon began to discuss a possible production in Kyiv; and in a Zoom call last August Mr. Benyuk asked me if I would come and direct it. I was flattered, and honored.

Being here in this beautiful city, at this time, working with these wonderful actors, has been a profound and wonderful gift for me. And how incredible and thrilling for me to see theatres full at such a difficult time. Thank you for inviting me.

My stage manager is a sweet young woman, but there is a confusion because the title 'stage manager' seems to mean something very different here than what it means in America or the UK. After weeks now, I'm still not sure what her job is or what she thinks it is. She works for multiple shows at the same time, is constantly leaving rehearsal for some reason. She never comes to rehearsal early, usually she is late, so I do all the setting up.

My Servilia talked to me about her brother, a wonderful actor/director who works at or runs another theatre outside of Kyiv. She is constantly on the phone with him trying to convince him not to join the army and to use his gifts as an actor and stay working in the theatre.

This kind of pressure—to sign up—is everywhere, on every man of military age. I'm sure if I were to ask, it would be a big topic and become a painful and difficult discussion.

Sunday, March 31st.
About 4:43am:

I'm in the shelter and it's been a very busy night: an air alert around 8pm while I was on WhatsApp with Cindy. It didn't last long, only about 20 minutes. Another around 11:30; I was woken up and came down to the shelter; this too lasted about 20 minutes. Then one around 4:30am. I don't even make it to the shelter before there's an 'all-clear.' I start back up, then fourth alert goes off, and so I am back down here.

5:11am:

An 'increased' air threat alert. I am still in the shelter, alone. Something feels different this morning. Or maybe I'm just very tired.

Morning:

I got out of the shelter after about 2½ hours. This morning on Telegram from the *Times of Ukraine* I read:

"Good morning Ukraine. Enemy mass shelling and the switch to summer time stole precious hours of sleep from us. We convert lack of sleep into donations, thank the air defense forces, and start the day with a smile. Let everything succeed."

It's a beautiful day. The sun's out, it will be in the low 70s.

I will get to rehearsal early today and work with my stage manager to organize the sound cues. I think this is something she does.

4pm:

Tired from last night's four air raids, but rehearsal went well. In Scene 6, Cicero attempts to convince Brutus that there is a way of life that is less engaged in politics or in war—the life of the mind. Cicero reads to Brutus the words he has created, adding to the language and the culture. Yulia, my translator, said that this was similar to conversations she has had many times with young male actors whose impulse is to join the army. She has argued numerous times that their abilities lie in being actors and making theatre, and they respond, but that is not what is really needed now. Yulia says this has been really frustrating for her.

My Cicero was in the Soviet army and served in Afghanistan; he is now 65 with bad knees. He'd love nothing more than to go back into the army, but with his knees he wouldn't be much help, he says. So the actor and the character here disagree, the actor feels that one's place now is not with books, or even with theatre, but fighting in the army. And the character thinks the opposite.

Later the same day:

The air raids are getting to be very common. After rehearsal, I go across the street to a little Ukrainian restaurant, order myself a meal, and the air-raid alert blares. I gesture to the waitress that I'll come back, and I head across the street to the theatre where a show is going on. The audience comes out of the theatre into the lobby. Chairs have been set up for this. I wait, and go back when it is all clear, to have my lunch or dinner while the audience goes back to the play they were watching.

A little before 6am:

I am back in the shelter. This is the sixth air-raid alert in the last 20 hours. Again something feels odd, like something is going on. I can only imagine what it must be like to have a child and you don't know what to do, and every few hours you have to go someplace or you have to ignore going somewhere. It must be intolerable.

WEEK FIVE:

Monday, April 1st.
1:45 pm:

A day off; I am sitting outside at the hotel restaurant; a magnificent and beautiful day, almost 80 degrees, crowds of people on the street. I just got back from lunch and speaking to my Cassius' class at the drama school; the biggest, most important, prestigious drama school in Ukraine, I'm told.

Walking there with Yulia (who would be translating), she explained how some male actors of military age are protected from going into the army. Institutions that the government considers 'essential', and these include cultural institutions like theatres, are allowed to keep 50% of their military-eligible male actors from military service. But it is up to the theatre to decide who to keep and who goes into the army.

I can't imagine the burden this puts on the people making these possible life-and-death decisions. She said it reminded her of my play when Brutus explains how Caesar made him choose which soldiers of his who had surrendered to Caesar would live and which would die. Brutus tried to find a reason for his decision: number of children and so forth. Yulia said it has been just that way with the theatres: who has small children or older parents.

We walk through the heart of Kyiv, through the square in front of St. Sophia's, down a lovely street full of shops, beautiful buildings. The beauty of this city unfolds itself day after day.

The school is in an old palace; we go up to the third floor; about 50 students are waiting for me. They are second-year students—out of four years of training. They applaud and give a kind of cheer or welcome 'chant' when I arrive. Immediately I am given presents: a framed award or certificate—I don't know what it says. A gold pin in a velvet box with, I assume, a famous person's face on it, probably the founder of the school; a book of photos about the history of the school over the last hundred and some years. And a cake. Later I receive a bottle of whiskey sent by Benyuk, who wasn't there. I have been told that he had to take his daughter and grandchild to the country—the air raids were driving them crazy.

The first question my Cassius asks is: was it difficult getting my wife and daughters to agree to let me come to Kyiv?

The students seem interested; questions about acting; one—how does a young actress get work? This question would be asked at any drama school in the world. I explain a little about actor agents—they don't have them here in Ukraine. They have casting agents, but not actor agents representing the actors.

I ask the question which was on my mind from the other day—why, ever since the full-scale invasion, are young people now so attracted to the theatre? I get a couple of answers: that the war has made them think about their nation, to see themselves as Ukrainian and that there's a long tradition of Ukrainian theatre. Theatre is one way to learn more about their culture and country.

Someone else says it is a wonderful distraction from the war; not in the sense of getting away from bad things, but allowing oneself to focus for a while on something else.

When we finished we had pictures taken. One young man asked Yulia if he could give me a hug.

Went with my Cassius and one of the school heads to a Ukrainian restaurant. We discussed among other things, *A Streetcar Names Desire* which this co-head is now directing. She said that in the translation Blanche is described as a "butterfly" but in the English it is a "moth." I said there is a difference; and I thought it's not so much how she looks that Williams describes, but rather he is alluding to the expression "a moth to the flame"—the flame, of course, being Stanley.

A slow walk, by myself, back through Kyiv.

I am now sitting outside.

Tuesday, April 2nd.

I woke up this morning to learn that my Brutus still isn't well; he has lost his voice, though he will do a performance in another play tonight, because the theatre cannot afford to cancel shows. But he won't be at rehearsal today.

I learn my Cicero is in the hospital with his knee problem.

There is not one moment in the play when either Cicero or Brutus is not speaking or being spoken to. So we'll see what today brings.

It's a hard play to do without actors.

Later that day:

Around 4 o'clock:

I ended rehearsal early. We got some things done; we began to work out the opening; I got to rehearsal early and sketched out an idea and we rehearsed that. I talked with my Porcia about her relationship to Cassius, because my Cassius was there. Syrus was there, so we worked on the two 'plays within the play' which this character performs.

My work, both as playwright and director, is all about relationships between characters. Right now my actors are acting with themselves or with me. I'm not panicked. We have plenty of time. But it would be more fun if all my actors were here.

Oksana wants to organize a masterclass for me. I will give her some ideas and work on that today. She made a lunch for us, a Ukrainian dish. I think she feels bad about my not having actors.

What I write for the masterclass:

In Conversation with American Playwright/Director Richard Nelson

An Actor-Centric Theatre.

At a time when theatre directors focus more and more on creating a visual language, Nelson, as both director and playwright, pursues a very different direction. For him, the actor/character is at the center of theatre, and the essential relationship of theatre is that between a live human being (the actor) and other live human beings (the audience) who share the same space at the same time. And so the expression, exploration, revelations, and perhaps interrogation of character (of human beings) is what theatre is all about. A seemingly simple aesthetic that has come to be seen as radical in our times.

Wednesday, April 3rd.

8:30am:

No air raids for three nights in a row. What's up?

6:30pm:

We broke rehearsal at 4pm and I have just had dinner. It was nice to have my Brutus back, and my Porcia. So I almost had my full cast, only missing my Servilia who will be out sick for the whole week.

I learned that I lose Porcia for Friday, Saturday, and Sunday because she is filming.

I lose Cicero tomorrow because it's his birthday, and for some reason that's considered a day you take off.

It's slow going; I think we did some good work; I think I did good work. The actors go in and out. This is not the sort of work they are used to; their first effort is always to 'act,' which is not what I am after. Then I talk to them and they seem to understand, they seem to take it in. It's going to just be two steps forward and one step back. I feel fine and I'm here for the simple reason of wanting to be supportive of the theatre and my art in Kyiv at a time of war.

The weather has been very warm; people outside in T-shirts, shorts; then the air got bad because of some kind of pressure from the Sahara that blew in some kind of pollution. People were told to stay inside. Then big winds blew the pollution away.

I'm going to WhatsApp to London in about an hour to check on how things are going there with my show.

To add to what I just said, being here at this time is about a lot more than making art.

Thursday, April 4th.
9am:

The air raids have paused for some reason, nothing again last night, and nothing yesterday. The Russians are bombing the hell out of Kharkiv, but staying away from Kyiv right now.

Rehearsals are tricky. I woke up this morning thinking maybe I should take an earlier suggestion to double-cast the two women characters, Porcia and Servilia. I say this because my Porcia told me only yesterday at the end of rehearsal that she would not be available Friday thru Sunday. I hadn't been told this and I'd asked everyone to give the company manager their conflicts so that she could share them with me. Porcia is in every scene of the play; I can't run any complete scene without her.

And my Servilia has been sick all week. I have seen her only one day in the last two weeks. She's just in one scene, so that hasn't been a big problem. Also I worry she isn't happy with the role.

So I got up this morning and reached out to Oksana, telling her my situation and suggesting that we double-cast these two roles. That would give me two actresses for each role, and so hopefully I'd always have at least one in rehearsal. I've never done this before; there are a lot of problems to it; it's not the way I like to work.

I really don't feel I'm in a position to tell actors what they can and cannot do; I come here as a guest, I come here at a very difficult time, to a very difficult place. I admire everyone for what they are doing. If they need to be busy, if they need to keep themselves busy, to maybe get their minds off the war and all that comes with that, it's not for me to criticize or judge. I simply want to adapt to what I'm given and to the situations that I find, and then work to deliver a production to the best of my ability.

About 6 pm:
After rehearsal:

I made the decision to double cast. I did this to stop having to jump around rehearsing the play with different scenes in different order. I need to go through the play scene by scene, in the correct order, and work out many problems that relate to that. I have a young actress coming in tomorrow to work on Porcia. I met her briefly, she says she's excited; she said she'd wanted to work with me.

I think that I'll have someone coming in for Servilia tomorrow morning as well. I'm not sure yet, I'm waiting to hear back from Oksana to see if the actress has agreed.

I think it's the right thing, and an interesting thing, but it will be challenging. I talked with Porcia who supports this. I noticed that after our conversation she focused better on the rehearsal.

No air raid today. This is a very long stretch and so it feels a little weird. Others have told me they feel the same.

Still Thursday:

The heating in the hotel and the theatre has been turned off. I'm not sure if this is because of the war, to save electricity, or if this is just the norm in Kyiv at this time of year. I think it is the war.

Friday, April 5th.
6:45am:

There was an alert last night just after I spoke with Cindy. Went to the shelter, was down there by myself, wasn't there for more than 20 minutes.

Woke up to a couple of reports from London about my show there. All very positive. This will be the first time in my career where I have missed the premiere of a new play of mine.

This morning I've got two new actresses coming in. I'll be working with them all day today.

6:40pm:

Very good day in the rehearsal room. Both actresses are named Maria and both are terrific. Honestly, so many of the problems I've been having with my Servilia and Porcia just didn't exist today; the two new ones jumped in without the questioning. The young Maria was introduced to me as 'Masha'. She then asked for me not call her that, because 'Masha' is Russian.

We worked hard, and succeeded in doing a lot of very good work. The new Servilia has known my Cicero for many years, and they are close, which is helpful to the scene they have together.

It was a very rich and encouraging rehearsal. I hope we can keep it up.

After rehearsal I had an interview with a young woman from an internet magazine. She had done her research, asked good questions. She was interested in my take on Ukraine and Ukrainian theatre, my knowledge of which is of course very limited.

Just as we finished in the lobby there was an air-raid alert. So I stayed in the lobby; and since the bar was open, I had myself a glass of wine, which was nice, a good way to wait out an air-raid alert. It went on for an hour and a half.

Oksana was also there, so we got a chance to talk and catch up. She talked about how her husband can tell just by the sound what sort of plane is approaching. She says this was going to be a long wait because planes have taken off, but now those planes have gone back, and new ones are taking off. Then she smiled and said, "see what we know, see what kind of experts we've become."

She talked about how in the early days of the full-scale invasion there was no electricity, and the theatre had various plans to keep open with generators. Of course the theatre doesn't perform during an air raid, but once one is over they can start. Once one of the actors in a show was caught on the other side of the bridge which closes during a raid and there was a great deal of panic waiting for him to get to the theatre.

I saw my assistant in the lobby; he said the Russians had hit 80% of the power grid of Ukraine, not sure that's true, I'll find out later. He said Odesa was down to two hours of electricity a day. And all across the country except in Kyiv.

Tonight is the first preview of my play in London.

Later on Friday:

My stage manager came up to me upset, saying that someone had been saying I was unhappy with her work, and was that true? And if so tell her and she'll do better. I said I wasn't saying that, but that the title 'stage manager' obviously means something very different here than what I am used to. She said she could do whatever I want and am used to. That would be difficult of course. I'll try to help her more.

Saturday, April 6th.
5:56am:

I'm in the hotel's shelter, alone, and have been here since the first alert at 4:10am. There was a second, increased alert, at 4:58am. I follow along with the Telegram reports: the most recent being that a cruise missile has entered Kyiv Oblast (the province surrounding Kyiv). This was six minutes ago.

Read the stage manager's report from London of the first preview of my play in London.

The response was warm.

This from Telegram six minutes ago: "explosions in Kyiv region, air defense working—monitoring public."

6:16am:

All clear, I head back up to my room. Is it too late to go back to sleep?

I read this on *Times of Ukraine* chat on Telegram:

6 dead and 10 wounded as a result of an enemy night attack on Kharkiv. The arrival of the Shaheds hit residential buildings: at least 9 high-rise buildings, 3 dormitories, a number of administrative buildings, a shop, gas station, service station, and cars were damaged.

4 people died and 25 injured due to enemy shelling of Zaporozhye. The occupiers directed 5 rockets at the city.

The rockets went to the target (Kyiv) with frequent changes of movement in order to complicate the work of air defense forces.

About 9:45am:

About to go to rehearsal when I remembered something that the new Porcia said yesterday. She was trying to find parallels between the play and Ukraine today. She said that maybe the characters were those Ukrainians in the Donbas who had and have supported the Russians. I hadn't thought of that.

About 4:30:
After rehearsal:

I spoke briefly with the director of my London show; she had a few questions.

Very good day of rehearsal with the new Servilia and Porcia. Worked on Scene 4. I thought it was going to be a difficult scene, but it worked out in an interesting way. Scene 5 feels a little long, but that's the only thing I worry about with it. We didn't get very far with Scene 6, Cicero, and Brutus. We'll pick that up again first thing tomorrow, and then go onto, hopefully, Scene 7 and Scene 8; if so we will have gone through the whole play this week.

I spent the morning working out a detailed draft of a schedule beginning from next Tuesday to the opening and sent it to Oksana. I have asked for a production meeting on Tuesday. I am used to the production manager calling these meetings; but there seems to be no production manager here. So I am on my own.

I'm tired, I got very little sleep, because of the air raid and initially waking up just thinking about the play.

Sunday, April 7th.
7:30am:

I answer a series of questions by a journalist:

Interview: Richard Nelson

It is a great gift for the people of Kyiv that you personally came to stage the play and support us. Tell us why you decided to do it.

Actually, I see this as my receiving the gift—the gift being the opportunity to work here, make theatre, in this theatre, this city, country, at this time. I've been working in the theatre for a long time, and it is a very special feeling—a gift—when what you're doing or trying to do (make a play and production) seems to have real meaning, value, and purpose. Making art, any sort of art, in a country that's being attacked can be an important response, I think, to such attacks.

This is your second staging of this play. What will be your directing accents this time? [By which I think she meant, will I just be copying the previous production or adding new things?]

I last directed this play in 2008; I'm a different person than I was then, so if for no other reason the production will be very different. But a play set in the summer of 45 BCE, outside Rome, will certainly have new meanings, new connections today, in Ukraine. And no doubt they will rise to the surface in places and ways that I have not expected or anticipated. My play is a series of 'conversations' between characters—Brutus, Cassius, Cicero, and others—but it also is a conversation with the audience—and how an audience today in Kyiv will listen, what they will hear, and how they will make connections to today—this greatly interests me.

How did you choose the actors, what is important to you in working with them?

Various actors were videoed answering questions I had submitted to the theatre; and I watched these videos and tried to put together an ensemble. Of course most of the actors spoke Ukrainian in these videos, and I do not speak Ukrainian, so what I was watching was tone of voice, body movement, etc. But mostly I was looking for actors who were not 'acting,' who were just talking to me through the camera; as this is what we are hoping to achieve in the performance as well.

How has your stay in Ukraine affected the production (perhaps you will have some research or plan to add certain moments that resonate with Ukrainians, will be tangential to our history or realities)?

This is a very interesting question. Do I add lines, moments that have specific resonance? I don't know yet, but probably not. The play is already very much about today—about a dictator, and those who have allowed him to become one, and the compromises they have made, and the delusions they hold—until it all becomes clear to them what they have become. And, maybe, what they must do. I think an audience can find in this story, and with such characters, many very specific moments that resonate today. Though the play is a 'history play', I do not write such plays to dramatize interesting history; rather, my interest is to use history and historical characters to somehow address the world as I see it today.

5:50pm:

Another fine day with my new Porcia. We worked through the whole play in order! We had one guest watching—we've had a number of actors come in to watch rehearsal—and at the break we talked.

The guest asked me why I was here, what I was doing, was I scared? She said that I reminded her of Woody Allen directing, because of my mannerisms. I think it's possible he's the only other American she's ever really seen do any directing. I don't know. I continue to sort out my casting issues, hopefully I resolve these in the next few days.

Beautiful day, and it is only going to get more beautiful over the next few days. I hope to wander around a bit tomorrow. Maybe head in the direction of St. Sophia's and into the neighborhood where I was last Monday talking to the students.

A few minutes later:

Another observation that I've been meaning to record: on the street it seems like there are far more women here than men. More than double, if not three times as many. You see groups of women, three, four, five together. And in the theatre as well; I would say that at least 60 to 70% of the audience are women, if not more. I suppose this too has to do with the war.

WEEK SIX:

Monday, April 8th.
4:15pm:

Our day off. I took a walk this morning, first down the hill to the bank and to the stationery store to buy a few notebooks for rehearsal.

I walked back up to the top of the hill and visited the National Museum of Ukrainian History. A huge building, protected by sandbags; I was pretty much the only person there, except for the older women who sat in the various galleries as, I suppose, guards.

I've been many times to the Imperial War Museum in London; one of my plays, *Goodnight Children Everywhere*, originated from such a visit when it had a show by the same name, about the children evacuated from London during the Blitz. One incredible thing about the Imperial War Museum is that, with full British irony, it is located in what had been Bedlam insane asylum. This great museum is actually misnamed, it should be called the Imperial Anti-War Museum because after even a single visit you come away with a profound understanding of the horrors that war can bring.

Whereas the Imperial War Museum charts the horrors of wars past, the National Museum of Ukrainian History seems to have dedicated itself to the war that is now going on. So it is a museum about today; I have never before experienced anything like this.

The first things you see when you enter are smashed military equipment, road signs with bullet holes displayed almost as art objects, or at least as historical objects with descriptions:

The scorched earth of Kyiv region was literally strewn with burnt enemy equipment and mutilated remnants of the occupiers. The exhibition is based on materials collected by the museum staff in the Kyiv region, mostly in the Irpin area. It is dedicated to the heroic defense of the capital of Ukraine, the ancient symbol of which was a bow or crossbow. Eternal memory to the heroes who sacrificed their lives defending Kyiv and Kyiv region!

A wall of photographs of one destroyed town, Borodyanka:

The Minister of Internal Affairs stated that Borodyanka is one of the most destroyed settlements in Kyiv region. Bombs were dropped on 9-story buildings. Rocket fire from planes demolished high-rise buildings to the foundations. People were buried alive in the basements that became mass graves. There was no military facility here. Columns of tanks and armored personnel carriers of the occupiers shot people who were trying to dig up the rubble. The occupiers did not allow the bodies of the executed and tortured men to be taken away for burial. It should be noted that villages around Borodyanka were no less affected by the Russian invasion. The photos are of destroyed houses, smashed cars, scattered around the ruins of toys, sledges, belongings.

One wall was dedicated to the "Occupation of Irpin," located only seven km from Kyiv, and specifically to its bridge over the Irpin River connecting with Bucha.

After its destruction on February 27, 2022, people crossed the river on boards. This exhibition presents the stands of the Heroes of the Anti-Terrorist Operation, a piece of the bridge, belongings of the evacuees smashed to pieces: a crutch, scooter, damaged taxi emblem, hand truck, first aid kit, homemade white flags made of rags and bags.

In the first room I went into was a display of armaments used to defend Ukraine, going back to the Vikings; so bows and arrows and hatchets, then to the Middle Ages, the 19th century, through the failed war for independence in the early part of the 20th century until the weapons used against Russia today.

A list of names and photographs of all the employees of the museum who are now in the military:

The National Museum of the History of Ukraine is proud of its employees who joined the Armed Forces of Ukraine, National Guard, and the Territorial Defense of the Armed Forces and work tirelessly as volunteers.

The staff of the Museum is sincerely grateful to the colleagues who despite the humanitarian profession, became defenders of the nation and the state. They defended Kyiv and Donbas, liberated Kharkiv and Kherson regions, save lives, and provide the front with everything necessary. Despite the difficulties of military service, soldiers-museum workers help to enrich the museum collection with artifacts of today's war.

In the next room were objects stolen by the Russians and later repossessed.

After walking up a grand staircase, I found myself in a room with hundreds of photographs of soldiers. These were men and women killed at the siege of Mariupol. Each had a small biography, and in front of some were fresh flowers.

From here I walked down into a reconstruction of a cellar, or what was labelled as a 'concentration camp.'

Having occupied Iahidne, the Russian military forcefully herded the local population to the basement of the village school, which turned into a real concentration camp. For almost a month, 368 people were kept there, including 69 children. The youngest child, who was kept there together with the others in a room with a total area of 197 square meters, was one and a half months old, and the oldest hostage was 93. The space in the basement did not allow people to lie down to rest, they could only do so in turns. To the right of the exit, a list of the dead was being recorded. To the left of the exit, the names of those who were shot.

Displayed here were objects left behind: a baby's booties, a child's toy.

I have been here now for over five weeks; and visiting this museum was the first time I found myself on the verge of tears.

As I said, I was probably the only person in this entire, huge, four-storey museum, so I could be alone with my thoughts. I sat and watched videos of today's war. I returned to the photographs of the museum's employees in their military uniforms.

I sat there for a long time.

I took a long walk into Kyiv, stopped by a bookshop, had a coffee; visited St. Michael's Cathedral (he being the patron saint of Kyiv).

I got a message from Oksana that she had arranged a meeting with my designers, so I hurried back to the theatre. Together we worked out schedules for tech-ing my show. I am trying hard to be clear and express what I need.

I had lunch at a restaurant, right up the street, with a view of Kyiv. They had a 'Fasting Menu' for Orthodox Lent, which was entirely vegetarian. So I was pleased. I had a cauliflower steak.

Wednesday, April 10th.
Around 7:30am:

No air alerts last night, I woke up thinking about something from rehearsal yesterday. My Cicero asked me if "the government was back." At first I didn't understand, then realized he was asking if the House of Representatives was back in session. He asked if I thought they were going to send weapons to Ukraine. I said I wasn't sure, but then I said, "yes, I'm sure they are." He said, "we need missiles!"

His son-in-law is a soldier heading to the front; his daughter lives in Kharkiv, which is bombed daily. His mind is very much there, as well as on Washington.

Thursday, April 11th.
Around 7:15am:

I just got out of the shelter after 3½ hours down there. First the alert and then the extended critical alert. This time I wasn't alone. First I was joined by two young Ukrainian women in their late 20s; they spoke English. Then another couple came in with the front desk man, who had brought them down and then left. The second two are on some kind of tour; they weren't a couple but somehow friends. She is Ukrainian and he is from the Netherlands, I think. They were going somewhere for some reason. They kept talking about train and bus schedules.

The older woman said I looked familiar. She asked my name and then she and the younger women all Googled me.

They camped out and tried to sleep. The older two organized places on the floor, on the rug; and slept or tried to sleep. One of the young women stretched out along some chairs with a blanket over her.

The other young woman and I talked for a long time, maybe a couple of hours. I never got her name.

An interesting, smart woman; she and her friend live in Bucharest. She works for a Ukrainian company that sells building equipment—obviously it is not doing very well now, but there's the anticipation that once the war is over, there will, obviously, be a great need for such equipment. From her I got a better sense or understanding of the Ukrainian diaspora, caused by this war—which by the way, everyone makes a point of calling 'the full-scale invasion' so as not to downplay that the war in fact had started years before.

Both young women were from Odesa.

We talked a lot about Odesa or rather she did—about the beauty of this seaside city, where she loved growing up; about her childhood there and her teenage years. She talked about going out with friends and dancing; about the beauty of the city in spring and summer; how she and her friends would go out in a boat.

She showed me videos and photos on her phone from her time in Odesa before the war: photos of her and her friends having fun, and videos of them dancing. Her 'life before the war'; displayed in front of me, there in a bomb shelter, in the middle of the night. It is what she wanted or needed to share, and I was there.

She spoke about the need to have a sense of humor; about a close friend who emigrated to Los Angeles and the difficulties she was having there, working 15-hour days. Her friend is a designer, but without a European or American degree in design it has been tough. She only recently got a job, or as this young woman called it a "legal job." The job she'd had before in LA was with an abusive boss.

This young woman wondered if her friend would ever come back to Ukraine; mused about the difficulty her friend had had, just trying to pay for food; how expensive things were in LA. She showed me a video of this friend in LA just dancing in her apartment, wildly dancing for the camera, her iPhone.

I got the sense that she was talking about herself when talking about her friend; about her difficulties, questions about her future.

The two young women had just come from Odesa where they stayed in the other young woman's apartment on the fifth floor of an apartment building. She made that point, "fifth floor." I suppose to show that it didn't feel safe.

She was interested in why I was here, what I was doing. I told her a little about my work.

When the alert was all-clear, and we left together, she thanked me for coming to Ukraine and doing this work. I'm sure I will remember more from our long conversation, but this is what I remember now.

Moments later:

I need to update things about rehearsal. I now have double-cast two of the parts. I am in a very tricky place; the two new people cast as my Servilia and Porcia are more right for the roles than the two I had originally cast. I know this, but as a double cast they will need to share the roles and share the two openings. I've never done this before. I've never had the experience of going into rehearsal and having to do everything twice. And where with one 'cast' it feels effortless, and with the other it is difficult. I'm not quite sure what I'm going to do, how this is going to work out.

I need to work through the entire play on, I hope, Saturday. I won't have the time in rehearsal to do this twice, that is, with each cast, so I am going to have to make a decision, and my decision I think is clear. I want the best cast to play the first time through so

I can see the play clearly to see where we are. I'm not sure what reaction that is going to get.

It's a funny bind to be in. I'm here to do my very best, to make the best piece of theatre, art, that I can make for this city, country, and for these incredible people at this time in a war. At the same time I see myself as a guest; I am here to watch, learn, and not cause any heartache or frustration or hurt to people who have already lived through such heartache and hurt. Those two ambitions are possibly in conflict right now.

Later that day:

A few more thoughts about my discussion with the young woman from Odesa:

She told me that her 14-year-old sister has now spent two years in Bucharest, and has developed friendships and a life, a life experience that is so different from the one she grew up with in Odesa. She has begun to see her sister as not really being Ukrainian or certainly not Odesan.

From her, I felt a profound wave of homesickness in our conversation; it was in the way she spoke of Odesa. Her grandfather had been in the Soviet navy, and had gone around the world twice and so to many places. He had told her: no matter where you go, no matter what new places you find, there is no place like where you grew up because there is something that holds you, connects you. People know you or they know people like you, so they understand you, your gestures, your thinking, and especially your sense of humor. She was implying that she has been cut away, taken away. I kept thinking of Nabokov's *Speak Memory*; that beautiful book about homesickness.

Later that day:

She really wanted or needed to share those videos of herself and her friends with someone, and that someone became me. I'm not sure why me, but we were in a shelter and I was listening.

It was as if she needed to tell someone "this is who I am, who I was, and still am. Here I am dancing with my friends, making my friends laugh, this is who I am, even though I'm not there now."

Still later:

This young woman speaks Ukrainian, Russian, English, Romanian. She told me she has just learned Czech. She wanted me to know, and she repeated this a number of times, that Ukrainians work very hard, especially when compared to people from some other European countries who seem more relaxed and expect things to be given them. This might have been to counter the cliché about Ukrainian refugees in Europe: that they don't work, and expect handouts.

She sees herself and her friend as working hard; her friend in LA works 15-hour days. She repeated this three times. At one moment, she wondered out loud if maybe her friend will meet a man in LA and never come back to Ukraine. She said that two or three times: "I bet she never comes back." She qualified this, saying her friend is not one of those women looking for a man to take care of her. No, her friend wants a career and, again, works very hard. But still she might meet someone; and that could even happen today, and she would never come back.

Was she also talking about herself? I think so.

So the Ukrainian diaspora: she is living this, with her friends; these twentysomethings. She showed me a photo of six or seven of her girlfriends: "that one stayed in Ukraine." "That one is somewhere else."

"That one is Russian and she's gone."

Sitting down in the shelter, I listened to a story of loss and homesickness, all told with a smile, a laugh, not a hint of self-pity; only toughness and so with grace and beauty.

Still later:

As I was talking to the young woman, here's what was happening at Odesa. I read that earlier today, four people were killed including a ten-year-old boy, and as many as 14 more injured. Four of those had life-threatening injuries, one man had both of his legs amputated. The attack happened in the evening rush hour, with people heading home, and then came a quick 'double strike' at those who had come to help the victims of the first.

Tonight on our nightly WhatsApp I told Cindy about this young woman, and she read to me from Maria Stepanova's wonderful *Memory of Memories*: about how Odesans are unusually tolerant, how they didn't expect people to assimilate, but to be able to hop from language to language, idea to idea. A very special unique place, with an unmatched cuisine. She quotes a Russian officer: "everyone is young and having more fun in Odesa."

About 9am:

I'm jumping backwards now. After rehearsal yesterday, which was complicated as I've mentioned, I met up with Oksana, who took me to an art museum. We decided to walk through the heart of Kyiv; once again a beautiful walk, past St. Sophia's, through what she called Kyiv's Central Park.

The museum was mostly closed, which is the case for most Kyiv museums now, because the art here is being hidden to protect it. There was one show by a famous contemporary Ukrainian painter, Ivan Marchuk. He's somewhat of a surrealist; our English-speaking guide called him the Ukrainian Salvador Dali.

A little later:

Marchuk has a complex history; mostly rejected and/or banned in the Soviet era. Once Gorbachev came into power, he was able to emigrate; he went to Australia and then Canada. After the independence of Ukraine in 1991, he received major awards and was given exhibits both here and in Western Europe. The guide wanted me to know that he was famous around the world. "World famous," she repeated this a number of times. Obviously it is important and needed right now for Ukrainians to feel they are known 'around the world.'

Oksana also took me to St. Volodymyr's Cathedral; another magnificent Orthodox church. A service was going on, a choir was singing. Oksana bought two candles which we lit to the health of our actors.

Over a brief meal, I got to know more about Oksana. She's been working in the theatre for about eight years; she first graduated school as an economist, then got interested in theatre. She speaks about the theatre in a very warm way: the actors are 'our' actors, while at the same time the they can drive her crazy. So from her it sounds very much like a family.

The theatre had been rudderless after the death of their founder; and the Culture Ministry ended up helping them sort this out. Bohdan Benyuk has been in charge for less than two years. He is a brilliant actor, she says; he knows everyone. The company manager has been at the theatre for 16 years. It is her life. She is 'the mother' of this company; knows everything, everyone, juggles everything, navigates the various problems that are constantly arising. I really have stepped into, and been welcomed into, a family.

We took a different route back; along on a series of stone paths on a ridge. It's like New York's High Line, if the High Line were on top of a ridge with a panoramic view of the city and river.

Lots of people out, gorgeous day in the 70s. As I said to Cindy last night, walking through this beautiful city, it seems unimaginable that someone would want to blow it up.

6:15pm:

After rehearsal:

All fine. Though complicated with my double casting. I still haven't figured that out.

Tired because I didn't sleep much last night because of the air raid.

I told Oksana after rehearsal about the young woman in the shelter; she said Odesa is known for its sense of humor. I said that's very much how she was. She found things funny. Made jokes.

Oksana asked if I'd ever been to Odesa, and of course I said no. She said it is beautiful, different because it is a sea town, except now you can't swim in the sea because of the mines.

I read this on the *Kyiv Independent* website:

Russian forces launched a massive aerial attack across Ukraine overnight on April 11, targeting critical infrastructure in multiple regions.

The Trypillia Thermal Power Plant in Ukrainka, Kyiv Oblast, was completely destroyed in the attack, the state energy company Centrenergo said. This led to the total loss of Centrenergo's generating capacity.

And I read this on the website of the *Kyiv Post*:

Ukrainian Air Defenses Fail, Russian Ballistic, Hypersonic Weapons Get Through

The Kremlin is ruthlessly exploiting Kyiv's critical shortage of Patriot air interceptor missiles: Russian ballistic and 'hypersonic' missiles on Thursday got through to targets mostly unscathed.

Russia's latest wave of missile attacks against Ukrainian energy infrastructure scored a victory on Thursday, with the Kremlin's hard-to-intercept 'hypersonic' and ballistic missiles punching through mostly untouched thinning Ukrainian air defenses to hit and damage power plants across the country.

Friday, April 12.

3:45pm:

After rehearsal:

Complicated day, and sort of a frustrating one. I didn't have my Brutus and there were only a few things to do.

I tried to work on the Servilia scene with my two Servilias.

Tomorrow I still plan to try to put the play together for the first time; because of the actors' schedules and conflicts, I have never had the chance to put even three scenes together in the correct order. I've had to bounce around. I don't think my actors understand the flow of the play yet, and how could they?

My plan had been to do this tomorrow and I will, but I learned that much of my furniture, which is my entire set, is being used in another show tonight and tomorrow, so I can't use any of it. I'll have to do sort of mockups of them. I suppose we can do some work that way, but that's not how I wanted to see the play, run through for the first time. Anyway, that's the way they work here. There are some very fine artists but they don't necessarily get the opportunity to be artists. It's complicated.

My translator could not come this afternoon, so my assigned assistant director came; he has rarely been around. He's a bright man, though seems to be unhappy; perhaps it's the war, I don't know. Right away he is questioning a piece of my staging.

My lighting designer came in, and he sort of lectured me a little about light; he said he too is a director.

Have I started to feel even more isolated, or is it 'ganged up on'? I'm hoping that tomorrow will be good, and I will see the play. Or—we'll have an air alert in the middle of the play so we will never get it done.

I will do it with the two new actresses.

Friends wrote last night about the opening of my play in London which seems to have gone well. Very pleased, though it feels very odd not to have been there.

Saturday, April 13.
About 6:45am:

I got up early, no air-raid alert during the night; though there was one in the evening just after I finished recording the last entry. It wasn't long though, just 20 minutes; again I was alone.

I read on Telegram that the destruction of the power station here in Kyiv the other night has caused a power shortage and there will be some sort of rationing soon, or maybe they're just asking people to use less, especially in the evenings. I'm not sure. I'll try and see what this means for me personally, if anything, and what it means for the theatre.

I woke up out of a dream: I was running down a hill of grass; and I knew it was Rhinebeck, so it was home. Like an image in a Mikhalkov film (a name one does not speak here because of his ties to Putin) where a child runs through lush fields of Mother Russia. Cindy was with me; we had decided to take a different way home, we followed on a path, passed a wooden house, then a cemetery. It was the kind of cemetery where after so many years they remove your headstone, and so you are forgotten. There was a name for this but I can't remember it. This temporary cemetery wasn't frightening, but actually felt comforting. Then we ended up at some kind of park, there was a place to buy ice cream; I had some money—including a 50 something coin, either a Ukrainian, Russian or Polish coin—and the woman selling the ice cream said she would take American money because that was where she was from.

4:42pm:

I finished rehearsal. I am recording this from the shelter. We just had an air-raid alert and warning of ballistic missiles, so I am here. Again alone.

We did go through the whole play—in order—today; and what needs to be done is much clearer. We did some of that work afterwards. I made some cuts with the actors; and we'll do a few more cuts tomorrow; not too much, I need to let them rest and some of them also have shows. Then we'll get back to work again on Tuesday—on our stage, with lights, sound, and costumes.

The play ran two hours and 10 minutes; I had expected two hours and 15. I think it will end up one hour 45 or one hour 50. I think there will be no problem getting to that. At least I hope so.

It was useful to do the play in order—useful to me, but also for my three guys, as they could now begin to chart the progress, movement, of their characters. I am here in the shelter, don't know how long I'll be here, but I have my computer.

9:20pm:

I was just about to go to bed, when I remembered a conversation I had with Oksana the other day—when we went to the art museum and then walked back through Kyiv. I asked her about the 50% rule; how cultural organizations and those other organizations that the government deems essential are given the choice of having 50% of their military-age males protected from service. And then, the heads of these organizations have to choose who goes and who stays. I asked if this was true, how things really worked, and she said yes, it was for some organizations though their theatre has been unable to get approval for having such a 50% rule. At the moment for them, it is worse; they can protect no one, so they never know who is going to be called up.

She told me that men of military age can be stopped on the street by recruiters or whatever you call them, and given notice to appear at what I guess is a draft board. The vast majority of these men who are pulled in are then immediately drafted into the army. So young men are scared.

I wonder if one reason why I see so many women on the street is because the men are scared to go out.

Sunday, April 14.
6:35pm:

A very short day of rehearsal, mostly just catchup, after the run of the whole play yesterday. We're making more cuts, tightening things.

Arman has returned from Paris to work as my assistant; I'll now have someone who works for me who totally understands what I am trying to do. He will be here through the opening.

He told me about his trip. He had to cross the Polish border where there were hundreds, maybe thousands, of people slowly going through the passport check, headed back into Ukraine; almost all women with children. There were a number of stairs and he helped with many baby strollers. They looked anxious, he said.

Maybe this is the week the US House of Representatives will vote for an aid package for Kyiv. Reports are getting darker here. I read that the head of the Ukrainian army says that the defenses on the front could collapse. There is a lot of talk that Karkhiv could be a target to be taken by the Russians, which would be a huge blow. It is the second largest city in Ukraine.

There are worries, understandable worries.

Life goes on, and we're putting on a play.

9pm:

In an interview earlier this week I was asked if I intended to change anything in the play to reflect the situation in Ukraine. I said that that was a very good question, and I hadn't really thought about it, but doubted I would. But today in rehearsal, while making changes, we discussed a line where Cassius says Caesar is sending soldiers out to the provinces to basically grant Roman citizenship to those people, thereby extending the boundaries of Rome. We tweaked that a little bit, saying how Caesar was sending soldiers out to territories that had been conquered and forcing Roman citizenship on the people there. This of course is what Putin has been doing in the occupied territories of Ukraine.

WEEK SEVEN:

Monday, April 15th.
6:40am:

Day off. Slept through the night. No air-raid alerts.

I remembered a conversation I had yesterday with one of the young translators who has been helping out. She said how for a lot of people going to the 'theatre' poses a problem, they worry they wouldn't know how to behave, and so feel uncomfortable. For them it is not really their place. She said about my play—that when it is working well, in the first few scenes for instance—one feels that the characters are just people, and so not something 'important' and so not intimidating.

She said her father would never go to the theatre if it weren't for her and her mother—he being one of those people who feels it isn't his place and so feels uncomfortable. He worries about how he should dress and behave. I asked her what he did; he is an ambulance driver for the military, though fortunately, for now at least, he is assigned to Kyiv. And thank God, she said.

In my production here, including actors, designers, stage manager, and translators: I have four Marias, two Dashas, and four Sergeys.

5pm.

I just got back from the Kyiv Museum of Theatre and Film. A lot of things were not on display, but the second floor was devoted to Les Kurbas.

As I mentioned earlier, he was a very significant theatre director; seemingly influenced by and perhaps eventually also influencing Meyerhold, though I could be wrong. At least this is what the photos of his productions showed.

He was part of the Ukrainian cultural movement in the 1910s, at the time of the Russian revolution, when Ukraine tried to proclaim its own independence. The guide at the museum explained how Ukrainian theatre in the Ukrainian language had essentially been banned by Tsarist Russia; productions in Ukrainian being limited to light comic shows or folk plays. The museum displays the official Russian proclamation. No serious or dramatic work in the Ukrainian language could legally be performed.

Pretty much everything in the museum, like pretty much everything in every other museum I've been to in Kyiv, tells the same story: Russian oppression of Ukraine and its culture. This is the repeated story. Understandably.

Les Kurbas was fired from his theatre in Kharkiv, then the capital of Ukraine, for anti-Soviet views. Invited to stage a production of *King Lear* at the Jewish Theatre in Moscow, he started work only to be arrested, put on trial, and sent to the camps.

There was an exhibit about his trial. He was sentenced to five years hard labor, and sometime near the end of his sentence, he and other intellectuals, Ukrainians, in 1937, were taken out into a field and shot.

While in the camp, Kurbas produced plays for his fellow inmates.

He is considered the father of modern Ukrainian theatre; as major a figure as Meyerhold, or Jacques Copeau or Granville Barker.

Why didn't I know about him?

In 1920, Les Kurbas directed *Macbeth*; the first time that any Shakespeare play had ever been performed in Ukrainian. Oksana said this was a very big moment in the history of Ukrainian theatre, in fact, it is now seen as the beginning or dawn of Ukrainian Modern Theatre. It was performed in country villages, during a great famine. The company played schools, outdoors; bartering their performance for food.

Kurbas played Macbeth himself.

Tuesday, April 16.
6:30pm:

After rehearsal. Our first time in the theatre with lights and sound, though no costumes yet.

I got to the theatre early to talk over cues with the lighting designer who was surprised that I wanted lights today. I had

had a production meeting (which I called and ran as there is no production manager). I had sent out a schedule, which I thought made clear what I was doing or hoping to do. Why was he incredulous that I wanted lights? I don't know.

15 minutes before rehearsal the costume designer texted to say she had gone shopping and would bring all the costumes tomorrow.

My plans seemed to be falling apart.

My designer quickly set up some lights; we got some cues written down.

Seeing my frustration, one of my Porcias said to me, "welcome to Ukraine." She explained that it always feels like "nothing is happening, nothing is happening, then suddenly everything is happening."

I asked the head designer here why there wasn't a production manager overseeing us at this stage? She smiled and said, "no, there isn't one." So everyone is on his own and in my case, how one coordinates without knowing the language is tricky. Anyway, we got through the day and made decent progress.

My Syrus wants to organize a party for me at his house where he has a swimming pool, and—more importantly—a Labrador Retriever. Next Monday, on my day off, I've been scheduled to give a press conference, so maybe after that?

Towards the end of rehearsal with us back in the rehearsal room for the afternoon, we had an air raid, and so we gave up for the day.

I went down to the lobby/shelter and hung out there. And now—another alarm has just gone off as I am writing this, so I will head back to the hotel shelter.

Wednesday, April 17.
About 7:30am:

I woke up thinking I should write a summary about the story with my first Servilia.

I cast her off a video to play Brutus' mother. We've had a bumpy time. She's been ill, as have others; she's been very busy touring another show around Ukraine, so has been unavailable for many rehearsal days; other times she's been off filming. I worry that perhaps she agreed before she knew the part. The part is only one scene. I have wondered whether she feels the part is too small or maybe that she is not right for the role. Early in rehearsals she nearly said as much: she expressed confusion at being the same age as my Brutus, who is supposed to be her son. At the time I tried to be helpful and encouraging; she has a mysterious and very interesting look, and I think could pass for anywhere between 30 and 55. And a charismatic face; a tall imposing woman. I thought it could work.

But she has come late to a lot of rehearsals and in rehearsal she requires a lot of attention. She is prone to making dramatic statements; she never seems to prepare. When she was sick, and also needed two days off for her husband's 50th birthday, as I've written, I took the opportunity to double cast the role with an older actress, one who is the right age for the role. She's been wonderful and seemed to understand the role immediately. Within two days she had learned her lines. I've never given her a note. Suddenly her one scene made total sense.

I wrote my first Servilia on Sunday saying I thought I should just go with the other actress. I apologized, because after all she had been right about the age of the character. It was my mistake. I think she was surprised and probably initially upset; but she wrote me a generous note that night saying she understood and that she too agreed "this is for the best."

I tell myself again, I am here to support these extraordinary people, these artists, during a time when their country, their city, is at war. I am trying to do what I can, which is to make theatre with them.

It is my way of supporting them, my way of saying that the value of theatre, of making theatre, is very deep and even profound. Even in the darkest times, theatre may become deeper and more profound (this is something I hope to discover). The last thing I ever want to do is come here and hurt anyone. But I found myself in a conflict between making the best art and trying not to hurt someone. I think I've gotten through it, we'll see.

A few moments later:

The new backstage assistant stage manager for my show is named Maria. So now I have five Marias, four Sergeys, and two Dashas working on my show.

9:15am:

Writing this from the hotel shelter. It is full for only the second time. A group of French people have descended upon the hotel, I saw them first at breakfast. And they are very loud, and shout at each other, totally ignoring the fact that someone else is in this small room and that maybe they should be more aware.

They shout on their phones, they shout at each other. Maybe they are nervous, I don't know. They are taking photos, including of me, without asking; which is thoughtless as well. I suppose to put on Facebook to show their 'time in the shelter.'

I only hope they are here on some worthwhile mission, and not here as war tourists.

Certainly this has been my most uncomfortable time in the shelter. Now one of them reads the news on her phone to the others across the room, past me—literally shouting it, laughing. Simply obnoxious. There must be some sort of 'shelter etiquette'…

I read this on the *Kyiv Independent* website:

Russian forces launched a missile attack on the city of Chernihiv on the morning of April 17, killing at least 17 people, and injuring 60, including three children, the State Emergency Service reported.
Two of the victims died later in the hospital, the service said.
Explosions were heard in Chernihiv, north of Kyiv, at around 9am local time.
A 25-year-old female police lieutenant is among the killed, said Interior Minister Ihor Klymenko. She was at home on sick leave when shrapnel fatally wounded her, according to Interior Minister Ihor Klymenko.
"This would not have happened if Ukraine had received enough air defense equipment and if the world's determination to counter Russian terror was also sufficient," President Volodymyr Zelensky said on Telegram.

Thursday, April 18th.

About 7:50am:

I slept through the night, woke up on my own, and not by an alert, around 3am, thinking about rehearsals.

Yesterday we were able to tech Scenes 2-4 in the morning and worked 4, 5, and 6 in the rehearsal room in the afternoon. So we are making progress, with about two more weeks to go. In the morning both Porcias rehearsed; I let them decide who rehearsed what and when.

After rehearsal, Oksana and the managing director drove me to the train station to buy my tickets for the train to Warsaw. Neither of my credit cards was accepted, so we had to wander the streets looking for a bank with an ATM. A bit of an ordeal. Oksana was very positive throughout. She's a good minder.

In the car Oksana told me that my first Porcia had just written to everyone on our Telegram chat that she had decided to bow out of our show. Having watched the second Porcia play the role that morning and seen how beautiful and right she was, she felt this was the right thing to do. She wrote that she didn't want to deny the audience the chance of seeing her. I was taken aback.

She also wrote how much she loved me and loved everyone, but that this was for the best. I thought we had started to find a way to work the double-casting of this role.

I'm not sure how much to believe, how much of what she wrote is true.

I wrote asking her just that, as well as saying I appreciate what she said. I told her how moved I had been by her video back in September, in which she spoke, in English, about the significance of my coming to Kyiv. I told her I'd shown this video to Cindy and that it had moved both of us. I asked if she was okay. As I've said before, I have not come here to hurt anyone.

She replied that what she wrote were her true feelings.

There was a lot of talk yesterday morning when people arrived to rehearsal about the air alert, which was a serious one, trains were delayed, people got stuck. A city not very far from here, to the north, an ancient city, older even than Kyiv, was bombed; 17 people killed, many more wounded.

Friday, April 19th.
About 9am:

Air-raid alert in the night around 3:30am or 4am; down in the shelter for more than an hour and a half. A few of the French people came in; they're still here.

Did a lot of emailing down there; didn't hear that anything came to Kyiv; so just a warning. Also devised a rehearsal schedule for the rest of my time here. We'll see what the day brings. Though I feel a little tired because I have been working since 4am and I'm already tired and it is not quite 9 o'clock.

I find myself writing to my friends and repeating: "nothing is happening, then nothing is happening, then everything is happening." Not quite the organized way I like to work, but I'll see if I can push out the envelope a bit and get everything a bit more organized and ordered than that.

Around 7:20pm:

A longish air-raid alert last night, from 4am to 6am.

At rehearsal we teched through the rest of the play. My Syrus was in an odd mood, questioning everything. Arman asked him if anything was wrong, and he said—"my son is going to the front next week."

Benyuk stopped by rehearsal for pretty much the first time; he spoke with Arman as I was rehearsing. Arman said he wondered what it would be like for people seeing the backs of actors. I realized that even a very experienced actor like Benyuk hasn't worked in or watched a show in-the-round. In this production there will be only one row going three quarters around the acting area, and a larger seating bank facing the fourth side.

We finally got the costumes today, and they started to look good. It's been a long haul to get here.

I know I say this a lot to myself, but I think we're on track, though still with many actor scheduling conflicts, but I now think that we'll get there.

A little later:

I just read that last night or this morning when I was in the shelter, Dnipro, a large city in southern Ukraine, was bombed: seven people including children were killed, and 30 injured. The attack caused a fire in a five-story building. The center of the city had been targeted, as was the case with the ancient city north of Kyiv a few days ago. This seems to be a change of tactics—acts meant to intimidate.

The Speaker of the House of Representatives seems to have decided to risk his speakership and push forward a bill to support aid to Ukraine. The bill should be voted on this weekend. It appears to be on track to receive bi-partisan support and go back to the Senate and hopefully be approved there and signed by President Biden soon. A long time coming; too long.

It has been hard being here watching my country unable to see beyond its shores. History repeats itself; so like 1939, 1940, 1941, when American isolationism prevented us from seeing real threats to the world. Maybe this weekend will be a good one.

A little later:

Something else from today: my actors and others around the theatre keep saying that every time an air alert goes off, they now think, "Oh poor Richard, he's going down into the shelter."

10:36pm:

I write now directly into the diary, and so not recorded.

It is one of those nights. 40 minutes ago an air-raid alert; I went down to the shelter—only person there; the noisy French group has gone. After 35 minutes an all-clear. I make it up one flight of stairs when a new alert sounds, so I am back.

While Googling I read the theatre's announcement for my masterclass this week: "The venue is also a shelter so in the event of an air-raid alert the program will continue."

I also learn my Brutus and Mr. Benyuk will be part of my press conference on Monday.

The announcement for the Masterclass:

The Podil Theatre has prepared an incredible opportunity for you to attend a masterclass by the American playwright and director Richard Nelson.
When*: April 28 at 2:00pm*
Where*: Podil Theatre*
We'll be introducing our guest American playwright, globally staged writer and director Richard Nelson.
Richard Nelson will talk about his theatre orientations, share his own observations and work techniques, and also answer the question of what, in his opinion, the theatre of the future should be.
The masterclass will be held in the format of a conversation.
The number of participants is limited!!!
The venue is already a shelter, so in the event of an air raid, the event will continue!

The announcement for the Press Conference:

PRESS CONFERENCE OF THE AMERICAN PLAYWRIGHT RICHARD NELSON REGARDING HIS VISIT TO UKRAINE.

On April 22, at 12:00pm, a press conference of the American playwright Richard Nelson regarding his visit to Ukraine will be held.

Organizers*: Ukraine-Ukrinform Media Center.*

Speakers*: Richard Nelson—American playwright and director; Bohdan Benyuk—artistic director of the Kyiv Academic Drama Theatre in Podil; Roman Halaimov is an actor of the Kyiv Academic Drama Theatre in Podil, who plays the main role in Richard Nelson's play.*

Why is this interesting?

During the press conference, Richard Nelson will talk about the purpose of his visit to Ukraine, his experience of staging political plays. He will also announce his own masterclass at the Podil Theatre, share his impressions of working in Ukraine during the war, the peculiarities of working with Ukrainian actors, and share his own emotions from the capital's cultural life.

It is worth noting that Richard Nelson came to the Podil Theatre to support the Ukrainian theatre and its fans. Yes, the director and screenwriter will work in Kyiv for more than two months. During this period, he plans to create a performance based on his own play with the actors of the Podil Theatre, hold masterclasses and discussions for Ukrainian artists and theatre artists, as well as learn more about Ukraine.

During his stay in Ukraine, the playwright will present his own play 'Tuskul Conversations'.

For reference*: Richard Nelson is an American playwright, writer, screenwriter, director, and teacher. Winner of the Tony Award and a number of significant awards in the field of drama.*

He has about 50 productions, 10 film scripts and radio plays.

He staged his most famous plays in London (Royal Shakespeare Company), Paris (Théâtre du Soleil), New York (Playwrights

Horizons, Old Globe, The Public Theater), Chicago (Goodman Theatre).

The format of the event is offline (Hall 1).
Journalists will be able to ask questions offline (Hall 1).

Journalists are requested to arrive half an hour before the event. Accreditation of media representatives will be carried out before the event at the agency.

Saturday, April 20th.
A little after 6pm:

After the two air alerts last night, there were two more today at the very beginning of rehearsal and one in the middle of rehearsal. During the first alert, we were just about to start work in the lobby/shelter when the all-clear came, but we were in the middle of working on a scene when the second alert came. We went down, moved around some chairs, and tried to rehearse. Everyone is very game for that; everyone knows that this is what I insist on doing—going to shelters for every air-raid alert—and they are supportive.

Nice day, good work. Tomorrow morning I hope to run the play for the second time and we'll see where we are.

Just got back from a walk down the hill, had a little early dinner with Arman, and an interesting talk with him about politics. He is Armenian, and he has spent time in Ukraine working as an actor. He has friends and relatives in Ukraine; he speaks Ukrainian, Russian, and another five languages.

We talked about the complexity of the political situation here, because of the close historical and cultural connections between Ukraine and Russia. He described the two countries as brothers, where one brother decides to go off on his own, gets a wife, wants to have a life and the other brother is very angry about this. There are ties between the two that are difficult to ignore, as they are very much there; yet that is just what Ukraine is trying to do; cut those ties and ignore any common history and culture and so denounce everything Russian. He says this effort is just another form of propaganda. He sees the world in a fairly complex way. But I tell him that when one is being attacked, the finer or more subtle shades get lost, and one is left with a world that is in black and white.

Later that night:

Thinking more about my talk with Arman: what I wanted to say is: yes, there's Russian propaganda and there is Ukrainian propaganda, but they are not the same. One is the propaganda of someone who is trying to hurt a person, and the other propaganda is that of someone trying not to be hurt. Are these morally equivalent? I don't think so. So is it really fair to compare?

I have just written to ask him this and he has just written back:

> *Of course there's no equivalent between those two propagandas. I support Ukrainian people in his resistance to Russian aggression. Totally. But I'm deeply against all kinds of racism and nationalism. And it's too difficult for me to listen to some stupid things like ugly Russian Jesus and nice Ukrainian one etc. It makes me desperate for humanity.*

Sunday, April 21st.
A little after 7am:

I woke up to the news that the House of Representatives has passed the support package for Ukraine, after a long time coming. The Senate should approve on Tuesday. Biden will sign right away. This has been like a cloud hanging over me and obviously this country ever since I got here.

No air alerts last night.

5:50pm:

End of week seven of rehearsal. It hasn't been seven weeks of rehearsing, because of the actors' conflicts and other commitments.

I have just come out of a meeting, where I learned that these conflicts/commitments have now multiplied. I had hoped to schedule a number of runs and lengthy rehearsals for next week, but in the last half hour I have learned that on 'this day' I can't have the theatre, on 'that day' I can't have a number of actors. Some days for the entire day. It is hard.

I had a run today, which was in some ways encouraging and in some ways not. My actors are still not off book; though they no longer carry scripts but call for lines or 'text.' They have a ways to go to get this play under their belts. I'm not sure how much I can help with this.

It's because they're doing shows every night—or are in other rehearsals—while rehearsing this play; they don't have the time.

The run thru, which we had to do in the rehearsal room, was set for 11 o'clock and didn't start until 11:30 because our stage manager didn't show up. She texted she was running 20 minutes late; we waited. She arrived 40 minutes late after we had given up on her and started. I played the opening music cue on my phone, and made the 'transition' music cues with my mouth. A crude way to begin.

I think I've staged the play pretty well. I think it will look fine in the space.

There is good progress with my Syrus; he found his way, I think. I really like my Porcia, my Servilia. Porcia has questions and some concerns, but we had a good talk instigated by her after the run. She came into the production only about 10 days ago and so had missed a lot of the discussion.

My Cicero is getting very good, except when he doesn't yet know his lines; then he pushes and 'acts' and struggles. When that happens, others then react or respond in the same way.

My Brutus too struggles with lines. But when he isn't struggling he is brilliant.

My Cassius is good, though he has had to take on learning a large role in *A Midsummer Night's Dream*. So this coming week I lose him for bunches of time. He performs the *Dream* next Thursday. I learned about this half an hour ago.

The reason why he is now learning another role in another play—and this puts everything in perspective and reminds me of where I am and what is happening here—is that my Cassius is replacing an actor who has suddenly been called into the military. This performance of the *Dream* had already been scheduled, tickets sold, so replacing the actor became the priority.

I understand. I understand where I am and what is going on. I said to the company manager as we finished this scheduling meeting, "I will do my best." I will revise my schedule, try to clear my mind, and figure out exactly what I am doing, or what I can do.

WEEK EIGHT:

Monday, April 22nd.
Morning just after breakfast:

Kharkiv is being relentlessly attacked. There is a rumor that the Russians will try and take it.

This is very personal; my Cicero's daughter lives in Kharkiv; she has just now left to stay with her parents in Kyiv.

I read on the *Associated Press* today, a person in Kharkiv saying "before they would target our manufacturing buildings, now it is as though they are attacking civilians directly." That seems to be the case now in other cities as well. The article goes on to say that through all of this the restaurants remain full, people have gotten used to the noise of generators. In one restaurant there are two menus: for when there is electricity and when there isn't. They are trying hard to keep their businesses open, as if to show each other, maybe even themselves, that they are not tragic victims with nowhere to go, but they can still do something.

There were a number of Swiss at breakfast; large men, members of a caravan bringing supplies, weapons from the West? I don't know. I think I recognized them from about six weeks ago, so this hotel is probably their regular stop, going back and forth.

One man spoke English and asked me if I was on vacation. I said I was a writer and working in the theatre around the corner. He got into a big, silly 'theatrical pose', arm raised, put on a funny voice, and exclaimed: "Do you need actors?"

That was my morning.

A little later:

Walking out of the hotel, one of their trucks had a sign "Ukrainian Freedom Convoy." The truck had Norwegian license plates. So they weren't Swiss but Norwegian.

Tuesday, April 23rd.
About 7am:

Two air-raid alerts last night; the second was 'critical', I heard explosions as I was going down to the shelter.

The Norwegians were down there for both of them. The first at around 10:30 and the second at 3:30am. For the first they all showed up, for the second, one or two were missing, probably slept through it.

They speak English; and they are excited. They are in the middle of an adventure. They are older men and have a boyish quality about them. Their adventure, I learned, is to collect used cars and trucks in Norway, either by raising money and buying them or by getting them donated, and then they drive the cars and trucks from Oslo to Kyiv where they hand them over to the Ukrainian military. They have done this trip a few times already; so I did recognize some of them; one of them said he recognized me from March.

They are from different walks of life; one's a lawyer, another's a businessman, another is retired. They were interested in what I was doing here; I avoided talking about the play. It was 3:30 in the morning.

Grown up boys on an adventure.

One other gentleman was down there; a Canadian professor from Toronto who had spent time in Kyiv in the '90s and has come to give a couple of lectures on economics at a university here. Mostly he said he just wanted to see what it was like now, having been here in the '90s.

He too is a nice man; has the room next to mine and twice yesterday got a little lost and tried to get into my room by mistake. The second time he was very embarrassed. He's a little absent minded, I think, a professor with his 'head in the clouds'. He arrived at the shelter for the 3:30 air alert in his pajamas.

I didn't have a chance yesterday to talk about my day. I met Arman, Oksana, the managing director, and his assistant and we all drove to the central Ukrainian press office, which houses much of the press of Ukraine and is supported by the government. There we met Bohdan Benyuk and my Brutus, and the three of us, with Arman, gave a press conference.

We were filmed for YouTube. It was simultaneously translated, which was difficult for me: I had an earpiece in my left ear and Benyuk sat on my right. He of course is an actor and speaks quite enthusiastically, passionately, and often directly right at me; that is, a few inches from my right ear. So while he is speaking Ukrainian in my right ear, I am listening to the English translation in my left. Not easy.

Benyuk was very generous about my work, what I have brought to his theatre, and how important it is that I have come to Kyiv. A beautiful welcome. My Brutus spoke about our work in the rehearsal room, and of my patience, which I appreciated. I too think I have been patient, but I haven't known if that was recognized. So it is, it's just that my actors don't talk about it.

There were maybe six or seven journalists, all women. There was one gentleman, a very tall man, who spoke English; afterward he explained that he worked for an EU foundation supporting Ukrainian culture. He is also an actor. He heard I was giving a masterclass on Thursday and wants to come. So I will probably see him again then. The whole event lasted about 45 minutes; a sweet woman moderated; pictures were taken. Oksana sent me some.

Arman and I walked through Kyiv, about a 40-minute walk; we stopped by a bookshop. I came back to the hotel and spent most of the afternoon working on the half-hour talk I'm to give at the start of my so-called 'masterclass' on Thursday.

Today we will have all day in the theatre, with full tech. Except for a couple of hours on Wednesday morning, we will not be back in the theatre until Sunday night.

Wednesday, April 24th.
Just before 8am:

Yesterday we had all day from 11am to 7pm in the theatre, with lights and sound, and it was hugely rewarding. We got through Scene 4.

We are definitely making progress, and everyone is very focused. I feel much more positive than I have been feeling.

We had an interruption, an air raid, and went down to the shelter, or I went down and everyone had to follow because that's where I was. I gave notes in the shelter as we waited.

There were of course more little hiccups today. I just learned that my stage manager, who isn't really a trained stage manager, is not going to be in rehearsal today because she's sick.

When I came back to the hotel last night, I got an email from a friend telling me that my friend David E. had a stroke and lost the movement of his legs, though his mind is clear. David produced my first tour to Europe; he brought my work to Europe.

Last night the Senate voted for the aid package to Ukraine; Biden will sign today or maybe already has. I heard that the aid could be coming as soon as the end of this week.

Thursday, April 25th.

7:50am:

Today I have my 'masterclass' which will be, hopefully, just a conversation. I've prepared a 20-to-30-minute talk, describing what I'm trying to do, my actor-centric approach, how that manifests itself in my directing and in the choices I make.

Oksana has told me that a large percentage of the audience will be theatre professionals, the rest are theatre students; a few will be interested theatre-goers.

She asked them for questions in advance; the questions that came back were surprisingly and disappointedly general. I worry that I'm going to get way too 'into the weeds', give too much 'detail' of my working methods, when perhaps what this audience wants is something more general. So they will be bored or confused.

It will happen in the lobby around 2:30pm.

4:59pm:

I am alone in the shelter. This is the fourth air-raid alert we've had today. The first came at 10:30 this morning, which interrupted the start of my shortened rehearsal (shortened because of my 'masterclass').

My Cassius lives on the left bank of the Dnipro; he was on the subway when the alert sounded, and when that happens the subways are stopped and the bridges are closed. He was 40 minutes late for this very short rehearsal from 11am to 12:30pm. So this made us lose more than a third of our time.

We rehearsed a few scene changes, and there was another alert.

Then a third just before my masterclass. A group of elementary school children suddenly appeared along with the audience waiting for my talk. Worried, I asked Oksana if these children were part of my audience. She explained there is a school nearby and the school uses the theatre's shelter. They were soon moved to another shelter in the building, one even farther below ground, one I didn't even know about.

The talk went well, I think. At least 80% of the audience were women and I learned most were actresses, so they had a real self-interest in my 'actor-centric' view of theatre. Thankfully I got some interesting questions: how do I choose my actors? Did I find Ukrainian actors different from other actors I have worked with? etc. A few came up to me after; one young woman said she was studying acting and that she had come from Kharkiv today just to attend my masterclass. Kharkiv is of course under constant attack.

As always and everywhere, the war is in the room.

Our conversation about the Ukrainian theatre soon became about the need for it to distinguish itself from Russian theatre. And that it is important for me to know that Ukrainian theatre is not Russian theatre. Ukrainian theatre has its own uniqueness, its own history.

An older man, one of Kyiv's chief theatre critics (and Oksana's mentor at college), asked me how I felt about post-modern theatre; the visual theatre that is now dominant in Western Europe. Today in Kyiv, I'm told, this has become the direction of most young theatre directors.

Arman was there, Yulia translated, Oksana ran it. I enjoyed myself.

My worries beforehand did not materialize. I had prepared well. My audience seemed engaged.

I gave a few young actors my email address; they asked if it was possible to perhaps continue the conversation.

Friday, April 26th.
About 6:30 pm. After rehearsal and dinner:

Today in rehearsal a youngish woman from the production side/design side of the theatre brought in shoes for the actors and was very rude. She criticized one of the actors who came into the room with coffee. We've had coffee in the rehearsal room every single day since I've been here. She then moved one of our rugs around and elbowed Arman out of the way; she was very gruff. We ignored her.

Then sometime during rehearsal she texted Oksana to complain about us for having coffee. Oksana followed up with our stage manager (who, because she was late to rehearsal, hadn't been there when this woman told off the actor) about how we're not supposed to have coffee in the rehearsal room, in order to protect the rugs that we are using.

Our stage manager then interrupted rehearsal to read Oksana's text out loud. Chaos then ensued; with some of my actors venting real anger and frustration. I'm sure these are tensions that relate to living day after day with this war. The actors expressed their feeling that the artists in the theatre aren't respected and are pushed around. One of my actors said that ever since the death of the founder some individuals within the theatre have grabbed power or felt self-empowered to tell the actors, the artists, what to do, and how this has created real tensions and issues within the theatre.

Talking about all this with Arman after, he said he saw a connection to Soviet times where people denounced each other, informed on each other, instead of just trying to work things out.

I went to Oksana and said "come to the rehearsal room, I need help. It's a mess." She came and tried to explain how the theatre doesn't want the rugs to get dirty. I explained that the rugs were going to get very dirty because when the audience leaves at the end of the show they will walk on them.

This storm passed; I let my actors have a breather, then we moved on.

Scheduling rehearsals continues to be difficult. I lost my Cassius at 2:30pm; my Cicero was sick with a fever. He's not going to be in tomorrow either; the theatre cancelled the show he is in. My Brutus had been promised he wouldn't have another show during the final ten days of my rehearsals, but he has now been assigned a show on Sunday; the actor double-cast with him in a role broke his leg.

This afternoon and tomorrow I have exactly one actor available: Brutus. So we spent an hour and a half or two hours, talking through the play, line by line. This turned out to be a useful exercise. We only got through two scenes. Tomorrow we will meet at 11am, and continue this process to the end of the play.

I also had time to chat with him; and we talked a little about how we thought a Ukrainian audience today will respond to this play; how they will take the end, which calls for the death of a dictator. Will they know that historically this led to civil war and chaos in the Roman Empire? And if so how will they connect that to today and Putin and Russia? We didn't know.

The characters in my play are presented as complex human beings; the performances are complicated and human. The play is, in fact, a series of questions—as are all my plays. So will a Kyiv audience today be interested in questions and questioning? Or, being under attack, are they only interested in answers? In the blacks and whites and not the greys?

This would be understandable—they're in a war. It was an interesting, healthy conversation: trying to put what we're doing on a stage in the context of this war.

Saturday, April 27th.
7:45am:

I got up about 25 minutes ago. Two air-raid alerts in the night; one around 11pm for 45 minutes, and the second much longer from around 3:30am to after 6am. So I am tired.

The gentleman from Canada was there in the shelter for both, but he had to leave during the second—he had a train to catch I think. I don't know. He left.

Once it was over I came back to my room and slept for another hour.

A little later:

I had a dream this morning that I was in the lobby of a theatre where I was doing a play; I think it was the play I am doing now. Various people I know surprised me by coming to see it when I knew it wasn't ready. These included actors from the Théâtre du Soleil in Paris, where I directed a play in December. More and more people arrived when I noticed that at a corner table was Ariane Mnouchkine, the director of the Théâtre du Soleil. I went over and tried to explain that I was having trouble getting my actors for rehearsals, scheduling, and whatnot. She was consoling and supportive.

7:30pm:

Long after rehearsal and dinner with Arman. Another day with just my Brutus, talking through the play, pretty much line by line to see if he understands the intention, and reviewing the translation.

We are eight weeks into rehearsal and we're still making corrections in the translation, because there are still problems.

Even though the initial misbegotten translation was hugely improved by Larissa and her friend in Paris, they had had to make it in a great hurry. Throughout rehearsal we have constantly had moments of "oh, what does it say in the English—that's not what it says in Ukrainian." Even today we're making some changes in the translation.

Mr. Benyuk dropped by to say hello; to check in to see how I was. I think he heard that I had only one actor available for rehearsal; and I am only one week away from opening.

Everyone is coping, everyone in the theatre seems to be making the best of what is. Tomorrow will be interesting: I get back into the theatre with sound and lights and costumes in the evening. From Monday on, with one exception, I have everybody until we open. I think. I hope. We'll see.

A little later:

Because of the two alarms last night I didn't get much sleep.

At rehearsal, Yulia, the translator, Arman, and my Brutus all said the same thing again: when they heard the alarms, the first thing they now think of is "poor Richard is in the shelter, and he's not getting any sleep."

WEEK NINE:

Monday, April 29th.
7:30am:

I start the week and I'm not sure how it will end up. I'm not quite sure what shape we're in, in terms of the production. Hopefully I will have my first dress later today in the afternoon or early evening. Then I'll see or begin to see. I know there's a lot of work to do, and there's not much time.

I don't have Cassius for most of tomorrow, he is in another rehearsal, replacing another actor who has gone to fight in the war. I've given up having invited dresses because there is no time, I haven't had the actors.

I woke up in the middle of the night, thinking about all of this, how it will turn out and what I could do or should do. Right now I feel pretty sanguine, it is what it is. I'm happy to be here, working here with these people at this time. I just hope I can present my work, our work, in the best way possible to show people how seriously I have taken this adventure, not just to come here in the time of war, but to come here to make art, make theatre, while in a time of war.

We open this week. Larissa arrives today; Oskar Eustis, the artistic director of the Public Theatre in New York where the play was first produced, arrives Wednesday. He is an old friend.

A little after 9pm:

I'm soon going to bed. I had a drink and relaxed with Larissa.

It's been a complicated day of rehearsal. We went through the first half of the play this morning with tech; we're now in the theatre for good. We went scene by scene by scene, stopping after every scene. The work looked fantastic. I was stunned by how much the actors understood what I was after, and how much they were able to achieve. I couldn't have been happier. I thought—"Wow, we are on our way!"

We had our dinner break. Came back and had our first dress rehearsal. Everything they did beautifully earlier, they now did not do. It was all heavily 'acted', pushed, unfocused. Was it the weight of doing it for the first time all the way through with tech in the theatre? Perhaps they were just focused on remembering their lines. It seemed like that they were not talking to each other, no longer listening to each other. It was disheartening.

Tomorrow we'll do another dress in the morning; then I lose my Cassius (and my sound designer) for the rest of the day to another rehearsal and performance. It is not optimum to lose one of my leading actors a few days before we open. But it's the war. Actors are called to military service; their parts need to be recast and re-rehearsed. That's the world we're working in; and we accept it, even embrace it. That is going to be my attitude for the week; just embrace where we are, and I should just be pleased with that. I've had this opportunity to try and make theatre with extraordinary people in an environment that is very difficult.

I am off to bed, early, as always. I understand that I am just one or two middle-of-the-night air raids away from being completely exhausted for the rest of the week.

A little later:

There are so many times—and today has been one of them—when I have been so focused on what I'm doing, trying to do—trying to control the situation as a director needs to—and then I get hit by the thought: this country's at war. It is being attacked. Every night. People are being killed. The people here don't know what the future holds; don't know what is going to happen, and know they are dependent on others in other countries.

So stop complaining.

Tuesday, April 30th.
Morning, a little before breakfast:

I woke up in the middle of the night, around 3am; no air-raid alert, just thinking about the play and production, trying to figure out its rhythm, its structure.

I woke up anxious; I will put in a few hours before rehearsal in the theatre, and try to figure out how to talk to the actors, what 'sign posts' to give them. I do go through this with almost every show, when with my work it can feel like there is just nothing there to hold onto. So—I need to create 'sign posts.'

Given that there is no financial reward for me, no fame, the only currency, if that is what one can call it, is the pride and desire to make the best possible art I can with these artists as they live their lives at this difficult time. That's it. I tell myself this in the middle of the night: that is why I am here.

Morning:

I am in the theatre alone, beginning to organize the day. I've written notes, clarifying the characters, for the actors. I have a meeting with the lighting designer at 10:30; I also reached out to the sound designer (both are 'Sergey') but I am not sure what I communicated.

Here is what I wrote him, which I translated with Deepl:

"Can you be in the theatre at 10:30 when I meet with Sergey (lights)?"

Here is his answer, also translated through Deepl or some other translation app:

"Dear Ritchard. All right. The driveway will be right next to me."

I responded with a thumbs up icon. A little tiny piece of what my life has been like here, putting on a play in Ukrainian.

7:30pm:

Just had dinner. Long day.

I got to the theatre very early. I totally re-did the music for the transitions, now using a musical motif from another show of mine. We worked on the lights, and eventually with sound. We did notes and then a dress rehearsal which—went well!!

I am infinitely relieved from where I was last night. They took my notes; talked to each other. Still a ways to go, things to do.

What a ride, and it is a ride. At the moment, I am relieved. 'At the moment.' We'll see what the next few days bring.

Tomorrow we are going to have a dress rehearsal with a small audience of actors from the company. I am also trying to schedule a photo dress for Thursday afternoon before the press preview, which I've just learned is when all the critics come. This snuck up on me. The theatre's plan was to have photographers shoot throughout this press preview, as well as having TV filming parts of the play. This sounded like it could be distracting; especially given that this would be the first time for the actors in front of a full theatre and that ours is a very 'quiet' show. So I have suggested a separate photo dress, and then a quiet, photo-less, performance for the press. We'll see what happens, as with everything.

I worked hard, I was up early; I was up in the middle of the night, and then up again early. I feel my actors are behind me. I know I've said this a million times: we'll see.

9:30pm:

I went to the hotel restaurant for dinner; because it is Lent they have the fasting menu, which is vegetarian; and I'm mostly vegetarian. I ordered the cabbage steak again. Afterwards, I told the waiter it had been delicious—and since I've been here nine weeks I've gotten to know this waiter well—he just looked at me like I was crazy. I guess he's not a vegetarian.

Wednesday, May 1st.
About 8:30pm:

We had our one invited dress rehearsal this afternoon, almost a full house—actors from the company and students from Benyuk's school. The response was strong.

And most importantly, afterward Benyuk spoke to me at great length about how important this production is and my being here has been. He said this play is about Ukraine, and Ukraine today; how everything in the play relates to what is happening, what has happened over the past ten years in Ukraine: the compromises made by people, decisions made while trying to sort things out. The play is about today.

This is everything that I had hoped for, everything my gut told me could be possible. He thanks me for being here, for bringing my work. He talked about three other openings in Kyiv these past few weeks. An *Othello*, a *Mary Stuart*, and the musical *Cabaret*. How they are all just big 'shows', not human, not about people, where the visual dominates the people. He said what we have created here is something human. Again that is what I'd hoped to do. He was articulating back to me what my ambitions have been. I am feeling very good right now.

Benyuk is not only one of Ukraine's most famous actors, but he has been a politician. He was a member of the legislature at a time when it was very contentious and when deputies were literally fist fighting with each other. He knows his way around; he is part of the birth of this nation (or rebirth).

He said to me and publicly to my actors: "how is it possible that someone from so far away, America, could articulate to us what we are going through?"

I can't say enough of how moved I was by Benyuk's response. And the response of others. One actress from the company hugged me after; she had been crying.

We still have work to do. I have a rehearsal scheduled for the morning.

Surprise! There has been a mix up with the schedule for tomorrow. The press preview had been set for 6pm, with all the press coming. Today we learned that my Cassius has another performance in another play at another theatre tomorrow also at

6pm. This mix up isn't his fault, he had told the company manager about this some time ago, but the information somehow got lost.

When Oksana arrived at rehearsal this morning and I told her this, I thought she was going to cry.

A lot of scrambling has now been done (by Oksana), and the press preview has been moved to 4pm tomorrow; my Cassius will then race to the other theatre, where in that play he doesn't enter until around 7pm. Oksana said if an air alert delays us, she doesn't know what we'll do, how we'll finish. We have moved our photo dress to 11:30am.

Oskar arrived earlier today; I will have a drink with him in a little while. He'll watch some rehearsal tomorrow and the press preview.

Thursday, May 2nd.
7:50am:

No air raid last night. There hasn't been an air-raid alert for at least four days—the longest stretch since I have been here. Though of course the Russians are attacking other places, especially Odesa right now. Fingers crossed as we go into these performances.

I had a good long talk yesterday with both my Brutus and Cassius about their scene in the play. We are going to rehearse it this morning. We talked about Caesar being Putin; so that when Brutus returns from a summons by Caesar, to think of having been called by Putin; and how it is Putin who has taken this special interest in Brutus. Brutus then has come back from Putin/Caesar to talk to Cassius, wondering if maybe there's a place for them, a chance to have influence. When put this way, the play gains something visceral. One of the first things Brutus says when he comes back from Caesar is that Caesar wants "no more war." I said to my Cassius, what if Brutus had come to you saying "Putin says invading Ukraine had been a mistake, let's stop this foolishness." Wouldn't you be interested in knowing more?

Friday. May 3rd.
A little after 7am:

A busy day yesterday; and a good day. We had our press preview, which followed a photo dress.

The photo dress was useful, though we started almost a half an hour late because the costumes had been washed, but not dried. How that happened, I don't know. The scheduling of everything has been up in the air.

Amazingly Oksana managed to move our two scheduled performances at the last minute. Fortunately, there were no air-raid alerts, which would have made finishing impossible.

Beautiful day. Beautiful weather. 70s. Not a cloud in the sky. Flowers in bloom.

A few things about yesterday:

I sat with Oskar during the press preview; he watched very closely, having reread the play, which he had produced in 2008, on the train. He seemed genuinely enthused and has already begun to discuss filming the play and streaming it at the Public Theater in

New York at some future date. He mentioned bringing this idea to the Goodman Theater in Chicago, which has a large Ukrainian population. If this does go forward I will talk to Théâtre du the Soleil to see if they too would be interested. Paris too has a large Ukrainian population; and the Soleil has been working closely with the Ukrainian diaspora there since the full-scale invasion.

The woman who runs the small theatre we're in, I guess you'd call her the head house manager, stopped me to say that though she wasn't a theatre professional, she considered herself a professional audience member and she's been going to the theatre since she was five years old (this was in Moscow). She wanted to tell me how important my play was and how beautiful. She wanted to thank me. She said she had seen these actors countless times in other plays but some of them she had never seen act better, never seen them do work of such depth as they do in my play.

Press preview went well. I didn't know who was there; Oksana had already told me that the press here isn't critical of the theatre right now, just supportive, as one would imagine.

In the 20 or so seats I could see—those circling around the stage—I counted 17 women. I'm not sure what that says; but it is an observation I've made before.

I met the writer, Andrey Kurkov, author of *Diary Of an Invasion*, which I read on the train on my way to Ukraine. A beautiful book; and I was able to tell him how much I had enjoyed it. He said a second volume of his diary is coming out, in English, in June. I'll get that right away. He has written many novels; he is probably Ukraine's most translated novelist. At least ten have been translated into English. I have read the most famous one, *Death and the Penguin*. Very nice to meet him, an honor; a significant Ukrainian cultural figure. Benyuk introduced us. Benyuk is in a play at the theatre based upon Kurkov's novel *Grey Bees*.

My Cassius was heroic; besides doing two performances for me, he had a third that night at another theatre; all with an eye infection. At one moment in my play he accidently hit this eye; I could see him flinch in pain. This worked for the character, worked for the moment, but I felt for him.

Last night after dinner:

I wanted to take Arman out to dinner because he's been such a huge help, a Godsend. We wanted to sit outside, so I took him to the hotel restaurant, which has a beautiful outdoor space.

There we ran into Larissa and her friend who was very apologetic because she had been late and missed our performance. So her seat sat empty.

The theatre had been packed; and given that we were overbooked, at my suggestion, Oksana added two extra seats, illegally—more than the fire code allowed.

Oskar joined us for dinner; he too is staying in the same hotel. When the bill came, he wanted me to calculate what it came to in dollars—for five people it was about $140. So he paid.

I have a little bit more rehearsal today. Scene 8. I will do notes on Scene 7, where my Brutus had tried changing what he had been doing, after discussing this with me. But after seeing it, I'm not sure it was right. Maybe we should go back to something closer to what we had. I will also clean up some transitions, and just spend time with these beautiful and wonderful people.

The first opening is at six. Second opening on Saturday at 2pm. And a party after.

It looks like it will be another beautiful day.

From Oksana on WhatsApp:

Dear Richard, I thank you for coming to Ukraine, to the Theatre on Podil. Thank you for staying with us and continuing our work despite all the experience and psychological stress. I thank your friends for whom another continent did not become an obstacle to attend the opening. Thank you for working with the theatre of personalities, preserving its original nature. I was afraid that without your watchful eye, the performance would change, but I see that you invested so much in the actors that over time they will only live the plot more confidently. I received many enthusiastic reviews, but most important ones for me: these two hours flew by imperceptibly, it was so interesting to watch the actors.

I would like to take this opportunity to ask you a few questions if you have time. If it doesn't happen, then it's nothing, it's beautiful because it leaves questions unanswered.

I wish you loud applause after a long pause. Back in university, we had a theory that the quality of a performance is directly proportional to the length of the pause after the final scene.

10:45pm:

It's late and I am tired and I will be brief. What can I say?

It was the first opening of my play and it was eventful. Three air-raid alerts in the evening, two during my play. The first happened in the middle of the third scene; and everyone, the whole audience, went into the shelter. It lasted about 35 minutes; we went back; a few people didn't come back—maybe they had babysitting issues or maybe they didn't like the first two scenes, I don't know.

The second air raid came with ten minutes left in the play. We didn't go to the shelter. Arman looked to me, and I shook my head. We hung on and finished the play. The first time in my nine weeks here when I broke my rule and didn't go to the shelter.

Then, having a drink with Oskar at the hotel restaurant, the third alert; I went to the shelter; Oskar finished his dinner and then joined me, and then Larissa came.

So we three Americans sat together in the shelter. Just us.

I was very proud of my actors; I told them after that they were heroes. It wasn't as good a performance as last night, by any means. They pushed more than they had, and more than I had watched them these last couple of days. They were trying to hold onto the audience; trying to find their way, and obviously, given the air-raid alerts, their minds were on other things. But they soldiered on and probably no one other than me would really know that it was different but I did notice.

I saw them trying to find their way back to what we had been doing, to the actual truth of what we had been doing, which they have found and felt. I watched them struggle to do this and at times achieve it; but it was an 'in and out' performance.

I said to them after, not just that they were my heroes, but that I was so honored to be with them, here, now. To work with them and make theatre at this time in these circumstances. I have watched how they do it, and watched how they survive. This is unlike anything I have experienced.

I was told it is very rare in the theatre in Kyiv for there to be two air raids during one performance; it has hardly ever happened in the two-plus years of the war. And never happened before during the opening of a play.

So a unique night, and a memorable one. But for now I want to say how proud I was today, that in the midst of this war we made theatre, we have struggled hard to achieve that. I cannot ask for more.

A little later:

I am going to talk to the actors tomorrow and again praise them for the way they make their work within the context of this war. I admire them, and have learned much from them. But I am going to ask them a question: do we push ourselves to make the best art possible in spite of this war? Or do we push ourselves to make the best art possible because of this war? If it is the latter then by pushing ourselves this way, we are in a sense fighting too. If it is in spite, we are trying to ignore the war. To make serious art at this time makes, in itself, a serious statement, of who we are, what we believe, and perhaps what the war is about.

Saturday, May 4th.
7:30am:

Got up about an hour and a half ago; not a lot of sleep, but no air raids.

I want to write down a few more details of last night's first opening.

It was a full house; not sure what it means to be an 'opening' as it just seemed to be a regular audience; maybe it only means the first time that people can buy tickets to your show. The invited dress with the acting company and Benyuk and his students seemed more like an 'event'; and Thursday's press preview seemed to have many more people who knew each other. So this was a different kind of opening than I am used to.

Oskar and Larissa were there. Oskar sat next to me; Larissa sat behind me. We had had a good day of rehearsal; making a number of little changes, tightening up the play, which I like to do; maybe lost another three or four minutes, shortening the transitions, getting everyone focused, and getting very close to the running time I had been hoping for.

The show opened on time, five minutes after six.

The actors had told me some of the responses they had received about the production; my Cicero spoke to an older theatre critic, who had called him in the morning and said how moved he was, and how he had nearly given up hoping to see such theatre again in Kyiv, where the post-modern director's theatre has dominated for some time. The critic was very excited; he told my Cicero that he had not seen him act so well since he was a young man.

Oksana told me there were good responses by younger critics as well. The feeling, the buzz, is that the show is successful, whatever that means.

From the beginning of the performance, I thought there was a little pushing by one or two actors; I think they were just excited about the show and wanting to do it well. But that could easily have been pulled back and I'm sure only noticed by me. By the middle of the third scene, a half an hour into the play, came the air-raid alert—my phone was on airplane mode so I didn't get the alert, but other phones did, and the actors continued until there was an intercom announcement from the theatre administration saying to take shelter.

Arman found me, asking how do we start again when the alert is over. I decided to go back and start the third scene again, because starting from the middle could be confusing. Went to the shelter; hung around with Oskar. The all-clear came after about 35 minutes; so the whole delay took about 45 minutes. I noticed that there were two empty seats in our row, and I noticed a couple of other empty seats; so four or five people chose not to come back for some reason.

When we got back I saw that the props were not reset for the top of the third scene; Arman and I started to reset the props; our stage manager having probably seen us doing this on her monitor came out and finished the job.

The play started again. I could tell that it was different; a different focus, the actors seemed distracted; so more pushing, trying too hard; it all felt a bit adrift and not as connected with each other as they had been. Every now and then they were connected, so they kept trying, but the interruption had hurt us.

I can only imagine what goes on in their own minds, when reminded so viscerally of the war; each has years of history with this war, their own private experiences. I can only imagine how difficult it is to regroup and do a play. But they got through it, until the last scene, which is only about eight minutes long. It had just started when the alarm went off again. I looked around. I saw some people in the audience who seemed not to know what to do. The actors ignored the noise and seemed to talk faster, move quicker, though with less focus. I could tell they wanted to be able to finish the play before the administration announced a stoppage. The idea of going to the shelter and coming back with three or four minutes left of the play would have been frustrating.

So the play ended; the alert was still going on; there was applause and people immediately stood and the actors tried to get me on stage, I didn't want to go; but my Brutus came and got me and I took a bow and was given flowers.

We then went into the dressing room; and we hugged, and I told them how proud I was. How they were my heroes. That was the evening.

About 9:30pm:

We had our second opening today at 2pm.

It was a beautiful show; the best show by far that we've had. In the middle of Scene 6 there was an air-raid alert, so we stopped. It was a serious one. Sometimes the alert is triggered by Russian planes in the air, but in this case ballistic missiles had been launched and were directed at Kyiv. We were herded into the lobby/shelter.

I assume the attack was quickly thwarted, and after a pretty short time, only about 15 minutes, the alert was over and we went back to our seats.

I wasn't sure how my actors would respond, but they stayed exactly where they had been and delivered a deeply moving performance. They spoke to each other; they listened to each other. It was simply the best performance of this play I have ever seen. What a beautiful way to end this time in Kyiv.

Afterwards there was a party; Oskar was there, Larissa was there. Obviously the cast; Yulia and Arman. It was a wonderful time; I felt wanted; people kept asking when was I coming back? Would I come back? How could I come back? I was given gifts; a Ukrainian Cossack shirt so I'm now an honorary Ukrainian, and other things—including a banner of the show with peoples' signatures, made by Oksana.

My lighting designer took me aside at the party, he wanted to tell me that he enjoyed working with me, and that he's thinking of going into the army. He said it feels so strange and difficult not to be there; feeling guilty, not knowing what to do, wanting to do things that were important. He has brothers in the army; one at the front, whom he hasn't heard from in a while. He spoke with tears in his eyes. All his gruffness was gone. We hugged.

Earlier, at rehearsal today before the afternoon's opening, I had asked my cast the question: is the reason we push ourselves so hard to make art to ignore the war or is it in response to the war? I think the answer I got—though not directly—was definitely the latter.

Sunday, May 5th.
9:30am. Orthodox Easter:

Met Larissa at breakfast; I said "Happy Easter." She said, "Christ is risen!" Larissa and Richard Pevear are both Orthodox Christians. Larissa has been to church, I think, every day since she's been here; there's an Orthodox chapel set within St. Sophia's where she goes.

I read in the *Kiev Independent* that the government has urged people not to go to church on Easter, and so as not to gather in big crowds, but to watch the service on TV.

Today we'll take a drive; my assistant director will pick up Arman, Larissa, and me, and we'll drive maybe an hour away to my Syrus' home, where he has organized a little party. My first visit outside of Kyiv—about ten kilometers away.

A thought from yesterday: as happened on the first opening; my Brutus got me out of the audience and made me take a bow with the company; then the company got Arman, then Yulia, and then Larissa on the stage to take bows. Larissa seemed so happy; she has said numerous times since that no translator has ever taken a curtain call!

I have a thought about writing a play for this company, for these actors. I am mulling over the idea. It's a place I'd like to come back to. We'll see. There's talk of a major Russian offensive coming later this month or June.

From Ariane Mnouchkine who wrote to Arman about our first opening:

Thank you, Arman. What a scene you are describing to me. I would have liked to be with you! Kiss Richard for me. And I had no doubt that he would get what he wanted. Despite the difficulties and dangers. Know that we all think about Ukraine every day.

Arman's talk to the actors before the second opening about the night before:

Maybe, what I have seen the night of opening show was the first time (I hope for the last time) that the theatre was so meaningful. Never before had the words had such meaning. The play was about Caesar but we knew exactly that it was about the war nowadays. It was a perfect fusion, a parallel between the play, the reality of the air alert, what the actors were saying and what they were feeling, the audience perfectly conscious about the real danger and wanting to stay and continue the show, to support the actors and challenge the enemy. I was watching Richard wondering if we must stop the show. Then I watched the actors and the audience determined to continue (to win?) And I said to myself, "in Rome do like the Romans do. And in Kyiv like the Kyiv people!" I was happy and grateful to have this opportunity to witness this miracle. Thank you, Richard.

From Telegram channel of Ukrainian Air Force:

On this bright holiday of Easter, we believe in the victory of good over evil, life over death.
On this day, we express our hope, support, and respect to our defenders. Who bravely fight against the evil with which the bloody aggressor attacked our country.
No matter how difficult it may be, mutilated but unconquered Ukraine will still shine as a successful European state!
I wish everyone peace and goodness. Believe in Ukraine! Help its defenders, protect and take care of your loved ones. Do not lose strength and optimism!
Together we will overcome everything!
Christ is Risen!

About 10 at night:
My last evening in Kyiv:

Spent the morning packing, taking a long walk. At 2:30pm went with Arman, Larissa, and was driven by my assistant director to my Syrus' house in the country outside of Kyiv. Took about 40 minutes to get there. No traffic.

He lives in a gated community, there was a guard.

Lovely large houses; his has a small swimming pool. He's been living there about four years. His wife, also an actress with the company, had come to some of our rehearsals to watch; a very nice woman. The food was a wonderful mixture of things, meats from a bar-b-que, assorted vegetables, salads. They gave us a tour of the house; they have two dogs. After all my time in the hotel, it felt special being inside someone's home.

There we met my Brutus; and Yulia. Others in the cast had family Easter obligations.

We had many conversations. The most moving—learning that this community bordered Bucha. So the first two months of the full-scale invasion, this community had been under siege. On our way there we passed the remains of check-posts still with sandbags. My Syrus' wife talked about what it had been like, hunkered down for those two months, with the Russians in the field just behind their house. The Russians had gotten that far. They had gotten to, what seemed to be, yards from their home.

There is an oil depository in the forest behind their home and they had prayed that a rocket would not hit it, as then the explosion would be huge and take down their home.

A number of homes in the community were hit by missiles; they have mostly been rebuilt or repaired by now.

I asked what they did during those two months; my Syrus' wife teared up, started to weep—two years later.

They went through a trauma, there had been no food. They heard on social media about a grocery store down the road that heroically, patriotically, had not closed during the assault. My Syrus' mother-in-law is in her 90s, she lives with them and needs special foods and medicines. The owner of the store filled bags with food and refused to take any money. Another neighbor two houses away brought them medicines from Kyiv.

Many stories like that.

My Syrus remembers sitting in his backyard when fragments from a missile hit his house. He had been sitting outside. His wife told him to get inside, and he said—"why? If the house goes up in flames we'll just have to go out again."

He told me about a neighbor he knew, "just a normal person, not a soldier" who had a rifle and how the man had asked, "did you see what was going on in the forest?" "No, what?" "I just shot and killed two Russians."

That was my visit to the country.

Beautiful day; stories of war and gossip about theatre.

Saying goodbye to my Brutus, he said to me how "this has been an incredible experience." And he thanked me.

When we left my Syrus said, "I love you." I said I'd come back.

The last thing my Brutus said to me was, "please thank your wife for letting you come."

A little later:

I learned today from my Syrus that before I came to Kyiv, he had serious doubts about being in my play. He had had two bad experiences with English directors. So he expected the same with me. He talked to Benyuk about getting out of the project; but Benyuk told him to hang around for a little while, give it time, and if he still felt the same way Benyuk would sort it out. So, unknown to me, that is how we began—with a lot doubts, a lot of questions

He also told me there were even actors around the theatre asking why the hell were they doing a play set in 45 BCE? So there was confusion and concern about even the topic of the play.

None of this had I known. I had walked into all of this innocent, and such innocence had been useful.

Monday, May 6th.
6:25pm:

I had coffee with Yulia, Arman, and Larissa; Yulia and I talked about what other plays of mine might interest Ukrainian theatres. I suggested a couple.

Oksana took us to a church where there were paintings by Mikhail Vrubel, an important Ukrainian painter of church art from the late 19th century, who was inspired by classical icon paintings. A very old church, first begun in the 10th century; over time it's been looted, burned, had its ceiling taken away for the iron, to use in some war, and abandoned. But here it is, again a church.

There are faded stucco paintings, and more recent efforts to restore or reproduce the earlier paintings. The church is part of a compound that includes a mental health hospital.

It is rumored that Mikhail Vrubel used patients from the hospital as models for disciples and maybe for Christ.

I learned that in Ukrainian people with insanity are called "God's people."

I learned the other day that after a cake is baked and sliced into, if there's a hole in it, Oksana's grandmother would say, "God slept there." Maybe this is only with the Easter cakes everyone bakes.

I learned more about Oksana. I asked how her Easter had been, and she got to talking about decorating eggs. She'd taken classes in this from age 12 to 20; and so had gotten very good at it. She said she'd taken photos of all the eggs she'd painted, but that those are now lost.

I learned that she had been living in Bucha with her parents when the full-scale invasion began, not that she had already left as I had thought. She didn't leave until after the first week. She convinced her parents to leave after two weeks, and they only took their winter clothes, the cat, and some coffee, thinking they would soon return. Oksana rolled her eyes at their bringing coffee, of all things.

While gone, their house was hit by a missile, caught fire, and burned to the ground. All of Oksana's childhood things are lost.

I hadn't realized any of this or the extent of the danger she had been in or her loss.

Driving back from the church, we passed through a section of Kyiv; Oksana commented that she had a friend who lived here; and, like me, he always went to the shelter in an alert—because it would get so loud. The area is often targeted because it has a couple of munitions factories.

We came back to the hotel area; went out to Oksana's favorite Ukrainian 'pie' store; then picked up our luggage at the hotel where Benyuk met me to say goodbye. He wanted me to write down my Rhinebeck address; he said he wanted to send me something. The general manager drove us to the train station; we found our compartments on the train.

I am on the train now, we just left Kyiv station. I'm looking out the window and watching Kyiv go by.

By around midnight I will be in Poland.

Tuesday. May 7th.
2:15am:

We have stopped at the Polish border; we will be here for a few hours as the train, somehow, realigns its track gauge. I slept for a few hours.

I remembered a brief conversation I had on Saturday during the second opening; when we had paused because of the air-raid alert, and were again taking our seats. A man came up to me to thank me for the play; he wanted to know how to get a copy, so I directed him to Oksana.

Then he asked: Why Rome? At first I didn't understand. He said, it's all about today, this is today, my play. I said it was also Rome.

Taking my seat, I thought of what I often say about theatre, and what a character in one of my plays says about acting: "what we do is see ourselves in others and others in ourselves."

I thought I could expand this to the question: why write and produce so-called 'history' plays—because they can help us see ourselves in the past and the past in ourselves. And so we know we are part of something not only greater than ourselves, but greater than our time in history.

8:15 am:
Poland:

Still on the train; a restless night but I got a little sleep. We were stopped at the border for about four hours; first I handed over my passport to Ukrainian soldiers, then the banging began to change the track gauge; two or three hours went by and I got my passport back, followed by Polish police to stamp passports. I was asked, in English, if I had any alcohol or cigarettes. The policeman asked me to open my biggest bag; I did, and he hardly looked inside.

Beautiful day. Blue sky.

I remember reading this before I left, and how now it has special meaning:

"I still remember the intense guilt I felt about being a guest in a catastrophe, a guest who could leave at will, because I lived somewhere else."

Yevgenia Belorusets, War Diary

Reviews of 'Conversations in Tusculum' at the Theatre on Podil, Kyiv, Ukraine:

NELSON FROM MALAKHOV'S GENERATION

The action takes place in Brutus' villa in Tusculum near Rome in 45 BC, about six months before the assassination of Julius Caesar. The characters are future conspirators. This is briefly mentioned in the program. If we knew nothing else about this story, this would be enough.

We imagine Americans, like the ancient Romans, very roughly, based on the films of the former about the latter. So you expect to be shown a Broadway show in a pseudo-antique setting, with a minimum of words and maximum dynamics. It's nothing like that. It's really just a lot of talking. For two hours, the conspirators just drink wine and talk. Nothing else. And it's hard to break away from that. We are so accustomed to something like this that it seems incredible. The playwright has a wonderful sense of presence, as if he wasn't constructing the play, but was in that villa and recording dialogues and fragments of phrases.

The play is remarkably reminiscent of Vitaly Malakhov's productions from the long ago, when the Podil Theatre had neither its own premises nor a decent actor's wardrobe. The actors sometimes appeared in front of the audience in everyday clothes, and the magic of the theatre came out of nothing, out of a live dialog between living people. Some of the participants in the play, such as Maria Rudkovska (Servilia), Serhiy Boyko (Cicero), and Serhiy Syplyvyi (Syrius), lived through those times. Others, such as Maria Demenko (Porcia), Roman Khalaimov (Brutus), and Artem Atamaniuk (Cassius), had only heard about them from their older colleagues. But the strange thing is that all six of them resemble the actors of this theatre as they were 30 years ago, as if they were just appearing on stage for the first time, without fame or experience, but honest with themselves and the audience. How does something like this become possible? Maybe it's the magic of the place—the performance is taking place in the old building where this theatre began. But how did Richard Nelson choose these particular actors (and he chose them not live, but from video footage), and how did they later feel like 'his' during rehearsals? Could it be that Nelson was from the same generation as Malakhov, who was unknown to him?

It seems that for the actors themselves it was a surprise that they succeeded. After the premiere, few people believed that there would be enough audience for such a long, purely conversational play. The sell-outs came later.

What attracts people to this production? Among other things, a kind of therapeutic effect. After all, now, in the third year of the great war, it is not so easy to reconcile oneself with the theatre, because it is sometimes embarrassing to watch comedies, and current dramas do not often talk about the war more than we have already experienced. And this play suddenly touches a rare string of the soul. It is a nostalgia for normal live family communication, something that is impossible for so many, and for which many of us would give a lot today. This nostalgia is so powerful that during the performance you repeatedly catch yourself thinking: even if I didn't know what they were talking about, I would feel good just listening to their chatter in this quiet house, illuminated by the evening light. This is something that is scarce in our lives nowadays, and in our theatre—maybe even less.

However, 'Conversations in Tusculum' is not what you would call an evening lullaby. We are looking at people who have suffered defeat but have not accepted it. Intellectuals who are not even concerned with what to do with the dictator Caesar, but rather with what to do with themselves in a situation where the homeland they loved is almost lost and, according to Brutus, there may be nothing left worth saving.

It's a kind of effect: you listen to the very family-like, very homely, even cozy dialogues of these people—and meanwhile, somewhere inside you, an alarming note keeps ringing. Because you know (and the program reminds you) that in a few months these intelligent people, at least some of them, will stop their talks, take up their swords, and stab the one who stole their homeland from them.

They will do it, and they will never return to this quiet house again.

Vitaliy Zhezhera, *Ukrainian Theatre Magazine*

This conversation isn't really about Caesar. Rather, it's about power, the escalation of conflict, finding one's place in the sun and ways to stop the war from ordinary people who are in an emotionally unstable state. This is why the performance resonates so much with the modern Ukrainian audience. We watch how the heroes experience fear for themselves and their families and worry about the country and the nation as a whole They sit down to decide how to defeat the dictator and save their future. The performance demonstrates universal human values, because almost each of us wants prosperity and a peaceful life—here a deep parallel is laid with our present life.

Dmytro Gelevera, *OBOZ.UA,* May 18, 2024

Light, smoke, music, costumes, projectors, moving stage, orchestra, play of light, scenery, and dancing. The vast majority of modern viewers now go to the Ukrainian theatre for a bright and beautiful picture. This aesthetic is completely destroyed by playwright Richard Nelson's psychological play, 'Tuskul Conversations,' which, with a minimum number of visual elements, focuses attention on the inner essence of a brutal dictator during the period of defining historical events.

In fact, psychological theatre is not a new style for Ukrainian drama. Despite the fact that now we gravitate more towards visual scenography than towards in-depth conversation. Listening carefully to actors who look like ordinary people is much more difficult than simultaneously contemplating the numerous effects. The audience closely follows the characters on stage and watches every movement from a close distance and, most importantly, hears every word. This is the ultimate task of psychological theatre, when actors do not act, but release heroes from their own souls.

To attract the viewer as much as possible, Richard Nelson chooses a chamber theatre stage, which is first 'assembled' by the actors themselves. It immediately becomes clear: the performance is not about flashy dancing, singing, and various effects. It is about deep involvement and the psychology of conversation, forcing you to penetrate into the state of mind and thoughts of the characters.

Theatrical magic with elements of psychological construction... Richard Nelson has brought this from another part of the world.

Valeria Muskharina, *Mirror of the Week,* May 19, 2024

EPILOGUE: 17 Months

An Accidental Director.

Over the course of 17 months, from January 2023 to May 2024, I directed three plays in three different countries, in three different languages. And I had a fourth play, which I did not direct, produced in yet a fourth country. My time in Kyiv is part of this 17-month-long adventure and so perhaps deserves some context.

In November 2022, Ariane Mnouchkine invited me to direct my play, *Our Life in Art* or *Notre Vie Dans l'Art*, at her Théâtre du Soleil in Paris, at its home in the Cartoucherie in the Bois de Vincennes, with her acting company. Ariane translated this play herself into French, a language I do not speak. I rehearsed for eight weeks in the spring 2023, then returned in November and rehearsed another month before opening the show in December.

In November 2023, the producer of the Hampstead Theatre in London asked to produce my solo play, *An Actor Convalescing in Devon*, in the Spring 2024, just a few months later. Clarissa Brown, an old colleague, directed the play, which was written for my friend, the actor, Paul Jesson.

In early September 2023, I directed a production of a new translation of Chekhov one-act plays called *Little Comedies* with the last acting company in the American resident theatre, at the Alley Theatre in Houston, Texas. The translation was by Richard Peavear, Larissa Volokhonsky, and myself. Richard and Larissa are the foremost translators of Russian classic literature into English alive today; and we have been translating Russian plays together for over ten years.

In the midst of this, I kept this diary as I directed *Conversations in Tusculum* in Kyiv from March to May 2024, in Ukrainian, a language I also do not speak or read.

For all of my life [beginning at age 15 and I am now 73] I have written plays—I am and see myself as a playwright. And for the first decades of my professional career I did not direct my plays, but watched others do that work. Then in the very late '90s I fell into directing—a series of happenstances really—and so I became, what I call, an 'accidental director.' It was never my ambition or aim, but something I simply fell into. And once into it, I surprised myself by enjoying it.

'Notre Vie Dans l'Art'; the Théâtre du Soleil, Paris, France.

I consider Ariane Mnouchkine to be the greatest living theatre director in the world. She built the Soleil literally from the ground up; 60 some years ago, she and colleagues squatted in the deserted munitions factories of the Cartoucherie, and over time built them into theatres. She is a strong woman; with an infectious laugh, an ironic look, and a motherly concern. The Soleil itself is more like a large family than any theatre company I had ever experienced.

Seeing only one production of mine in person in New York, and a few on video, Ariane invited me to direct my play with her company—why? She read my play in a night and decided she wanted to translate it. As far as I can tell, the only other plays she has translated are those by Shakespeare and the Greeks. She took me in at a time in my life when the theatre, the American theatre, had become mostly unrecognizable to me, and unwelcoming. I believe I was only the second director she had ever asked to direct her company.

The actors of the Soleil are well known and much admired for their physicality and musicality. Ariane productions are most definitely 'shows'—where the actors play with various styles of theatre, often from the Far East or Southeast Asia, wearing brilliant costumes, makeup, often even wearing masks. Ariane told me that what I do "is the opposite of what she does."

'Little Comedies of Anton Chekhov'; The Alley Theatre, Houston, Texas.

Something has happened in the American theatre (and probably in theatres in other countries as well) over the last few decades—staffs have grown larger and larger. Theatres that once produced X number of shows with Y number of staff now produce less, with ten times more staff. The cost of staffing, along with some very exorbitant salaries for those at the top, dwarfs the pay to artists. In other words (and I am certainly not alone in saying this) many large theatres have become institutions with huge numbers of employees whose singular focus is their own survival, above and beyond the creation of any art. They have become like ocean liners that now list to one side, and appear on the verge of capsizing. In Houston I would be working with the last resident acting company in the American theatre; a remnant of what was once a vibrant tradition in the American theatre.

Here I discovered another 'family', actors who have worked with each other for years, who have invested their lives and careers in a specific place—some have families, others have pets, many have houses, one or two live in apartments. They all wanted to share with me where to eat, where to shop, what to see—generous, often gregarious, talented people.

I arrived not knowing any of them (though at the very end of our rehearsals I learned one had auditioned for me over 20 years ago) and uncertain what I would find. I knew that the kind of production I was aiming for was very different from what the Alley, and these actors, had been doing. I could tell there was some skepticism, some curiosity—but these were actors who were confused about their place within the theatre, their importance, how they mattered. And of course, given that this is the last such acting company, they must have worried that they were the last remaining dinosaur, soon to be extinct. Again, these were people with families, and mortgages, kids in school, about to go to college. I felt their vulnerability and their questioning.

'An Actor Convalescing in Devon'; Hampstead Theatre, London.

During Covid I got a bit out of touch with a lot of people, including my friend and wonderful actor, Paul Jesson. And for a long time I didn't know about his illness—cancer of the jaw—nor of his ordeals with radiotherapy and all that that brought about. Then late summer 2022, Paul suggested we catch up on Zoom. By then he had written to me about his illness, and a bit about his recuperation. I have never asked Paul this, but I think he wanted me to see him, as he had changed, physically. And he was changed. The beautiful deep voice (I can still hear and see his magnificent Henry VIII at Stratford) was now quite different; certain words were tricky for him to clearly pronounce. We Zoomed for almost an hour; and I was moved by his matter-of-factness (not at all surprising knowing Paul), his acceptance, his strength as a human being. In other words, I found him inspiring. A few days later I woke up with an idea—why don't I try and write him a one-character play? I wrote Paul, suggesting this; of course he wasn't sure what I had in mind (at the time neither was I), but he also was intrigued.

An Actor's Theatre:

For all four productions during these 17 months, I approached rehearsals in exactly the same way.

I explained to my actors that what I was after wasn't 'naturalism' where so-called real life is somehow copied and conveyed. How I am after making something real happen in front of an audience. Not pretending, but true. To have actors really talk to each other and really listen to each other; not showing an audience this, but actually doing.

And I described each production the same: no 'set', only furniture laid out on whatever floor is already there; an early acknowledgement by the actors (or actor) that we are in a theatre—as they set up the furniture to perform the play. Nor were we going to do 'cinema acting', where again one pretends or 'shows' an intimacy, 'acts' being real, often to an off-camera person who is not completely participating. This is style, and I was after something else.

To each company, I told the story of my friend, C., a brilliant actor, with an extraordinary, probably photographic, memory. How I once directed him in a one-character play based upon a series of diary entries—a very difficult thing to memorize. How he would come to rehearsal and say, "give me a word, not 'the' or 'and'—but a noun and I will tell you what entry it is in." And so I remember saying "school" and he closed his eyes, thought, and then said, "which one, there are two." Soon after he performed our play in London, C. had a heart attack. He was revived, but too late, he went into a coma which lasted several days. When he came out of it, he had amnesia.

Sometime later, his sisters, both actresses, asked me to 'rehearse' him in the same one-character play; this time he would be reading it of course. 'Rehearse' had a whole new meaning because from one day to the next he didn't remember what we'd done. But he gave a performance, and watching it, we all were amazed and moved—it was as if he had never read what he was reading. He wasn't performing or pretending to read, he was actually reading to us as if for the first time. He read without self-judgement, without questioning; he was simply present. Here was an experience that I felt held a clue for what I wished to achieve in the theatre—a real event, not presented; something really happening in front of us, alive and true.

I explained to my actors that this was where I hoped we would be headed—real talk, really listening; human being to human being in front of human beings. Something alive and true.

I read them each the same quote from Anton Chekhov, a letter to his soon-to-be wife, Olga Knipper; she has obviously complained about the performance a fellow actor:

I wrote to M. to prevail upon him, in the letter, not to push his portrayal of a nervous man. A great majority of people are nervous, the majority of them suffer, a minority feel acute pain but where—either in the street or at home—do you see them throwing themselves about, jumping up and down or clutching their heads with their hands? Suffering should be expressed as in life itself, not with your arms and legs, but by a tone of voice, or a glance; not by gesticulating but by elegance. Subtle expressions of feeling are natural to intelligent people and must be expressed subtly in outward form too. The stage has its demands, [he is talking to an actress], you will say. No demands justify lies.

[Jan. 2, 1900]

For Chekhov, I explained, acting carried with it moral choices—to lie or to be true.

I quoted to each company a passage by the English director and playwright, Harley Granville Barker, whom I much admire:

One is tempted to imagine a play—to be written in desperate defiance of Aristotle—from which doing *would be eliminated altogether, in which nothing but* being *would be left. The task set the actors of it would be to interest their audience in what the characters were, quite apart from anything they might do; to set up, that is to say, the relation by which all important human intimacies exist. If the art of the theatre could achieve this it would stand alone in a great achievement.*

To *be* and not to *do*. Here I set our goal; to present real life—real human beings really talking and listening to each other; not pretending, not *acting* or *doing* or *showing*.

I explained that the route to the truth, in the theatre, always goes through the actor—not the director—and that character is the very heart and soul of what theatre is. The actor is at the center of my theatre.

I also explain something else to my actors as we begin to rehearse—and this is always met with some skepticism and so is only proven in the doing. I never wanted to direct my plays; I thought—and still mostly think—that playwrights are not good directors of their plays. However, about 25 years ago, through a series of happenstances, I fell into directing, and I learned something about my work that surprised me. I learned that when I write I do not see my plays—so I don't know how they should look; and I do not hear my plays—so I don't know how they should sound. Instead, I 'feel' my plays—they are like a dynamic—almost musical—and so I can close my eyes and 'feel' how a scene should play or how it was written to play. I explain all of this to my skeptical actors, who at first only see me as a figure with huge power in the rehearsal room, because I am wearing both the hat of playwright AND director. But power is not what I want; what I want is the actors' engagement, their perspectives, their feelings. And so I tell them that "we can try anything, because I don't know what we should do." HOWEVER, "I can tell when something feels wrong, and so when I say that, trust me, and then let's try something else." And in this way I found my way to direct my plays.

Initially actors are leery, but over time, hopefully it becomes a very warm and collaborative rehearsal room. I continue to deflect as much 'authority' as I can—I never sit behind a table—as if in some sort of 'judgement'—I constantly move around with my script; I rarely take an actor aside—but rather try and be transparent with my thoughts—because what I might say to one actor, could be useful to another. And so we begin to work by trial and error, and I try to put as few obstacles in the way of the actors as possible—again, the 'set' is really nothing, chairs, tables, rugs—which we can continue to reconfigure until we feel it's right. If I haven't said it enough, let me say it again: my theatre centers on the actor, and in rehearsal not to use an actor's thoughts, concerns, perspectives seems to me to be a huge waste of opportunity.

And I explained that our job is to be people on stage who are as lost, happy, sad, confused, ambiguous, etc., as any one person in the audience. AND—we will always fail. But that is the ambition, the goal; what we reach for.

I read off a list of what the actors will hear me say over and over again in rehearsal:

"This feels like a play."

"That's theatrical."

"You're acting."

"You're acting a character."

"Don't know what you are going to say."

"Don't know what you are going to hear."

"Talk to the person."

"Need to talk."

"Need to listen."

"Don't talk at someone."

"Ask real questions, not rhetorical ones."

"Who are you talking to?"

"Speak and think at the same time."

"Just be. Don't show or do."

As I have mentioned, I consider myself an untrained 'accidental' director; and I try and compensate for this by being well prepared. Before beginning rehearsals I will schedule each day—knowing of course that all of this could and probably will change (some scenes surprise one with the difficulty, etc., and there are actor conflicts—such as doctor appointments, illnesses, or far more complex issues as in Kyiv). But it is comforting to have a schedule, even one that will certainly change. And of course each day I know what I want to achieve, and I will have noted for myself at what time of the day we should have achieved what. In this respect, I suppose I am pretty anal. But having such a schedule allows me to be very free, open, and ready to listen and learn and rethink anything I thought I knew. Because for me that is what rehearsal is about.

When the World Feels So Profoundly Uncertain, Why Put on a Play?

In the midst of Covid, I wrote this article for *The Guardian* newspaper:

> *The director Peter Brook was once asked, "What is the future of theatre?" Without a moment's hesitation, he replied, "Tell me, what is the future of food?" In the middle of huge social upheaval, civil unrest, deep-seated injustice, and devastating worldwide pandemic [and today we can add incomprehensible wars] that have caused economic chaos and widespread personal tragedy, why put on a play? When the world feels so profoundly uncertain, why do theatre?*
>
> *There are of course different ways to answer these questions. There are many examples of theatre being a rich and entertaining expression of protest and ideologies, with theatre-makers putting to work their full range of theatrical tools for a specific cause. At other times, theatre has been a necessary escape from a troubled world; a momentary respite from conflicts raging outside its walls.*

It can also be something else entirely. There is a theatre that chooses not to be a participant on the battlefields but rather something running parallel to them. This theatre does not attempt to portray arguments being waged, nor does it allow itself to become a platform for them, but rather portrays characters who are simply trying to understand the world they are in, our world—as they ask themselves and each other: who they are, where they belong, and do they matter? While all the time they try and live their lives, that are perhaps more complex than any of the arguments circling around them. A theatre that is about trying to understand as opposed to one with answers. A theatre made up of questions.

The motto of La Comédie-Française is: 'Simul et singulis.' To be together and to be alone. In part this sums up the essence or at least the ambition of my kind of theatre: to bring together strangers, sit them in the dark, and have them grow together as a group; that is, to come together while being alone. When together, they find themselves with other human beings who also have families and problems that are universal, truths that are multicultural. There in the dark watching theatre together, perhaps they will come to feel, if only briefly, that they are not alone.

This is a good reason to put on a play in very difficult times: to share that in our confusion, our questioning and our self-doubts, we are not alone.

Rhinebeck, NY, June 2024

APPENDIX:

'Conversations in Tusculum' at Theatre on Podil Kyiv, Ukraine

Translated in Ukrainian by Valentina Zhigalova
and Larissa Volokhonsky

Brutus	**Roman Khalaimov**
Porcia	**Mariia Demenko**
Cassius	**Artem Atamaniuk**
Servilia	**Mariia Rudkovska**
Cicero	**Serhii Boiko**
Sryus	**Serhii Syplyvyi**
Director	**Richard Nelson**
Set Designer	**Andrey VonSchlippe**
Costume Designer	**Anna Shkrohal**
Lighting Designer	**Sergey Nevgadovsky**
Sound Designer	**Sergey Shevchenko**
Assistant Director	**Igor Mativ**
Assistant Director	**Arman Saribekyan**
Stage Manager	**Mariia Pantiukh**
Translators	**Yulia Sosnovska, Viktoriia Tsiluiko, Daryna Kryvoshei**
Deputy Stage Manger	**Vladyslav Tsekhmeistruk**

For Theatre on Podil

Artistic Director	**Bohdan Benyuk**
Managing Director	**Yevhen Syvnov**
Deputy Director	**Nataliia Chernenko**
Main Artist	**Mariia Pohrebniak**
Head of the Troupe	**Tetiana Antonova**
Production Manager	**Alla Miarkovska**
Head of Drama Department	**Oksana Prybish**
Coffee and lunch	**Yana Muzyra**

CONVERSATIONS IN TUSCULUM
Scene-by-Scene Synopsis:

Scene 1: Brutus and Cassius, while waiting for Cicero to arrive, share their fears about Caesar and their doubts about themselves.

Scene 2: Cicero, having recently lost his daughter, arrives and is surprised to be greeted by Syrus, an actor, who is Brutus' houseguest. Syrus fills Cicero in on Roman gossip; Brutus and Porcia greet Cicero. Syrus performs a monologue Brutus wrote in praise of Cato and his suicide in the face of defeat by Caesar.

Scene 3: As Porcia gets Cicero's new very young estranged wife out of his house so he can go back home, Brutus, Cicero, and Cassius confront their impotence in the face of Caesar's power.

Scene 4: Servilia, Brutus' mother and former lover of Caesar, has hurried to Tusculum after receiving Brutus' note hinting that he is contemplating suicide. She shares the note with Cicero who tries to convince Brutus that suicide is not a course to be taken, even though he too has often considered it.

Scene 5: Brutus had been called to Caesar's camp in the middle of the night; he now shares with Cassius his newfound hopes that they could still have influence over Caesar.

Scene 6: Brutus shares with Cicero his newfound hopes and gets Cicero to write Caesar a note, making an important gesture toward Caesar.

Scene 7: Brutus and Cassius return from a few days at Caesar's camp. They share with Cicero their humiliation, degradation and self-betrayals, the ridicule Cicero's note received.

Scene 8: After an evening meal, Sryus performs another play by Brutus for Cicero, Cassius, Porcia, which ends with 'he must die...'

PHOTOGRAPHS:

+	With Bohdan Benyuk	14
	The square at the bottom of my street	16
	The street with the old and new Theatre on Podil	23
	Burnt out & captured Russian tanks in front of St. Michael's	32
	The hotel's shelter	39
+	Rehearsal with actors	49
+	Rehearsal with actors	60
	The old theatre where we performed	73
+	Rehearsal room	78
	Signage riddled with bullet holes, Museum of History	86
	The theatre and our set	96
+	Cassius	100
	Poster for Kurbas' *Macbeth* (1920)	103
+	Cicero, Brutus, and Cassius	116
+	Brutus	126
+	Cicero	131
+	Syrus	134
*	With Oksana, Andrey Kurkov, Benyuk, and Arman	135
+	Porcia and Cicero	139
+	The empty stage	154

+ Photos by Lenka Kirichenko-Povolotska

* Photo by Oksana Prybish

All others by the author

ACKNOWLEDGEMENTS:

I WOULD LIKE to thank the entire staff of the Theatre on Podil in Kyiv, for their generosity, support, and inspiration. I wish especially to thank Bohdan Benyuk, its artistic director, for inviting and hosting me, Tettiana Antonova for helping me navigate my way through very complex rehearsal schedules, and Yevhen Svynov for his constant encouragement.

I wish to profoundly thank the actors of *Conversation in Tusculum*; much of this story is about them, their courage, difficulties, and their strengths. I also owe much to Yulia Sosnovska, my brilliant translator, and Arman Saribekyan, who came from Paris, stayed by my side assisting me, offering needed advice and listening to my worries. I also thank my designers, assistants, stage managers, and other translators.

Oksana Prybish was my gracious host and guide, who became my friend during my weeks in Kyiv. I deeply thank her for her help, humor, and amazing kindness. Her care for this project is woven throughout this diary.

Larissa Volokhonsky helped orchestrate the efforts to get the play produced in Kyiv; and she and Valentina Zhigalova saved the day by quickly completing a revised translation. Larissa has been part of this journey from the beginning to the end; I could not have taken it without her. I wish to thank Ostap Stupka for helping to bring the play to Theatre on Podil.

I need to thank the entire staff of the Vozdvyzhensky Hotel for taking such good care of me.

And I want to thank Susie Sainsbury for her invaluable and generous support which made this adventure possible, and the Marguit Grieser Fund and its head, Oskar Eustis, for its help.

I owe a great deal to my close friend, Colin Chambers, for his numerous readings of the manuscript and his insightful corrections for this book. And my thanks to Lucy George, the publisher, whose enthusiasm for such a book is deeply appreciated.

Finally I thank my wife, Cynthia, and my children, Avery and Jocelyn, for supporting me in this; I know it wasn't an easy adventure for them.

R. Nelson

Wordville

Milton Keynes UK
Ingram Content Group UK Ltd.
UKHW020650191024
449836UK00010B/134

9 781399 991964